PRAISE FOR

The Reluctant Leader

"Everybody talks about leadership, but nobody talks about the fear of leadership. Thank you, Pat, for knocking down the walls that keep so many talented people on the sidelines. Thanks to The Reluctant Leader, *taking charge isn't scary anymore."*

—Clint Hurdle

Former manager, Colorado Rockies and Pittsburgh Pirates

"History proves that a reluctant leader can turn out to be a great leader. The trick is getting past that initial fear. Pat Williams has crafted the perfect antidote to the hesitation that keeps so many gifted people from realizing their potential."

—Dave Clawson

Head football coach, Wake Forest University

"Leaders are often praised, but just as often, they are criticized and even attacked. It's no wonder gifted people are reluctant to step into the arena. Thankfully, Pat Williams sees the problem and has crafted the perfect book in response. The Reluctant Leader *is certain to allay the fears that are holding so many potential influencers back. I wish I had this to read as I moved up the ladder in my coaching career."*

—Dick Vermeil

Longtime NFL coach

"Pat Williams has written many great leadership books, but this one may just be the most important one. I read it with great interest and can highly recommend it to you."

—Jeff Van Gundy

Former NBA coach

"The Reluctant Leader *is a joy to read—and a book that only an authentic servant-leader could write. Pat Williams is that leader, and through engaging stories, lessons from personal experience, and a deep understanding of human relationships, he issues a call-to-action to step up and lead.* The Reluctant Leader *is full of sage advice, practical tips, and relevant examples that bring the text to life. Read it once just for pure enjoyment. Read it again to appreciate the wisdom of a legendary leader. Read it yet again as a guide on your journey from reluctance to acceptance of your own capacity as a leader."*

—Jim Kouzes

Best-selling coauthor of The Leadership Challenge*; fellow, Doerr Institute for New Leaders, Rice University*

"I have always believed in permitting our players to be themselves, to develop a culture of openness and trust. To do that you must identify those in the group who not only have leadership skills but who also want to lead. Some have the skills but for whatever reason do not step forward.

"I believe Pat Williams's book The Reluctant Leader *attacks this issue that hasn't gotten enough attention. Pat's book can be a dif-*

ference maker for those potential leaders who haven't taken that decisive step."

—Joe Maddon

Manager, Los Angeles Angels

"Some individuals are pressed into a leadership role without considering themselves as capable of leading. The Reluctant Leader *is the book that addresses this uncertainty. This book explores why individuals may feel unqualified for a leadership role, when in reality they are already leaders. Author Pat Williams, himself a one-time reluctant leader, explores how emerging leaders can learn what it takes to lead and, in the process, gain the confidence they need to serve others.* The Reluctant Leader *is an uplifting read, filled with memorable stories and practical insights. And for the record, even if you are already in a leadership position, you will find this book helpful and full of wisdom."*

—John Baldoni

Top 30 Global Guru for Leadership; executive coach; and author of many books including GRACE: A Leader's Guide for a Better Us *and* MOXIE: The Secret to Bold and Gutsy Leadership

"If you know someone who has leadership gifts but is hesitant to get involved, give them The Reluctant Leader. *It is the perfect answer to the 'stage fright' so many potential leaders feel."*

—Johnny Damon

Former Major League Baseball star

"Pat Williams's The Reluctant Leader *is a must-read for not only people interested in a career in professional sports but for anyone looking to become a true leader. Pat's stories and lessons from his long, distinguished career in professional sports are invaluable. Pat explains it all with a great sense of humor and humility. He went from a reluctant leader to one of the most respected leaders in all of professional sports. We can all learn from his journey."*

—Mark Murphy

President and chief executive officer, Green Bay Packers

"Finally, a book that deals with a problem that has been ignored for too long: the reluctance of a person with leadership skills to step up and get involved. Pat lays every fear to rest in a way that will instill confidence in the next generations of young leaders."

—Nick Nurse

Head coach, Toronto Raptors, 2019 NBA Champions

"Pat Williams is as prolific a writer as I have ever known. I have read perhaps a dozen of his books over the years. They have all been great reads about great leaders. But The Reluctant Leader *may be his most important book yet because it might just unleash some people who never thought of themselves as leaders. This book can shake them into action and charge their unseen leadership skills with potential they never recognized. In these times of global crisis, we need more great leaders.* The Reluctant Leader *will help make people who never thought it possible to become genuine leaders."*

—Richard Lapchick

Chair of the DeVos Sport Business Management Program; director, Institute for Diversity and Ethics in Sport; president, The Institute for Sport and Social Justice, University of Central Florida

THE Reluctant LEADER

OVERCOMING *the* HESITATION *that's* HOLDING YOU BACK

PAT WILLIAMS
WITH MARK ATTEBERRY

Advantage®

Copyright © 2021 by Pat Williams.

All rights reserved. No part of this book may be used or reproduced in any manner whatsoever without prior written consent of the author, except as provided by the United States of America copyright law.

Published by Advantage, Charleston, South Carolina.
Member of Advantage Media Group.

ADVANTAGE is a registered trademark, and the Advantage colophon is a trademark of Advantage Media Group, Inc.

Printed in the United States of America.

10 9 8 7 6 5 4 3 2 1

ISBN: 978-1-64225-259-0
LCCN: 2020922833

Cover design by Megan Elger.
Layout design by Wesley Strickland.

This publication is designed to provide accurate and authoritative information in regard to the subject matter covered. It is sold with the understanding that the publisher is not engaged in rendering legal, accounting, or other professional services. If legal advice or other expert assistance is required, the services of a competent professional person should be sought.

Advantage Media Group is proud to be a part of the Tree Neutral® program. Tree Neutral offsets the number of trees consumed in the production and printing of this book by taking proactive steps such as planting trees in direct proportion to the number of trees used to print books. To learn more about Tree Neutral, please visit **www.treeneutral.com**.

Advantage Media Group is a publisher of business, self-improvement, and professional development books and online learning. We help entrepreneurs, business leaders, and professionals share their Stories, Passion, and Knowledge to help others Learn & Grow. Do you have a manuscript or book idea that you would like us to consider for publishing? Please visit **advantagefamily.com** or call **1.866.775.1696**.

This book is dedicated to Jerry Steele. When I was a timid twenty-year-old at Wake Forest University, he saw potential in me and encouraged me to step up and become a bold leader.

CONTENTS

ACKNOWLEDGMENTS

I want to thank my writing partner, Mark Atteberry, for helping me write this book.

Also, as always, I want to thank Adam Witty and the support team at Advantage Media Group. They do a terrific job and are a pleasure to work with.

INTRODUCTION

The Journey from "Who, Me?" to "Why Not Me?"

Every book has a beginning, and it's not when the author sits down and types the first sentence. Long before that moment, there is thinking, researching, scribbling, jotting, outlining, crumpling, throwing away, and starting over ... often more than once. And even before all that, there is an event or an encounter, often arriving out of left field, that triggers a spark in the brain. A spark that can feel very one-celled and insignificant when it first flashes but that can over time grow arms and legs and hair and teeth. Any author will tell you that some of those tiny sparks morph and grow into full-blown ideas that simply demand, with growls and snapping jaws, to be reckoned with. They won't take no for an answer.

This book began with just such a spark.

It happened at a book signing I was doing in Orlando. Smiling people were coming through the line one by one, sharing the typical pleasantries. Suddenly I found myself facing a man with a much more serious expression. He got right to the point: "I've just been given a leadership role that I don't feel equipped for. I don't see myself as a great leader. I'm not comfortable giving orders. I don't like holding people accountable. I hate being in charge. Yet I've been given this responsibility, and I can't get out of it. Mr. Williams, you're looking at the most reluctant leader there's ever been. Do you have any advice for me?"

I did.

I told him about the time I too was thrust into a leadership role for the first time. I was in the Monogram Club at Wake Forest University. Less than a week before the club's annual freshman-varsity basketball game, the club president jabbed his finger in my chest and said, "Williams, you're in charge of the game."

"Who, me?"

"Yes, you."

"But the game is less than a week away," I said. "Surely everything has already been taken care of."

"Actually, nothing's been done yet. You need to get the tickets printed, hire someone to sing the national anthem, book the pep band, find someone to do a halftime show, and get started on the promotion."

At that moment I would have said *I* was the most reluctant leader there had ever been! To this day I have no idea why the president picked me. I had never been in charge of anything like that before. I can only assume he saw something in me that I didn't see in myself. So I did the only thing I could: I knuckled down and went to work. On game night a huge crowd showed up, and yes, all of my hastily—and desperately—made plans came together perfectly. I'll never forget going to bed that night thinking, "How about that? I'm a leader!"

The man at the book signing listened carefully as I shared my story, looking slightly more hopeful as I progressed. I wrapped up by saying, "Many people take their first leadership steps very reluctantly.

They tell themselves they don't have the time or the qualifications or the experience. And sometimes they're right. Not everyone has leadership potential. But I'm living proof that such reluctance is often unwarranted and can be overcome."

His next words struck the spark.

"You ought to write a book for all of us reluctant leaders."

For years that idea sat in the back of my mind. Then it began to morph and grow, finally demanding to be reckoned with, which is why you are holding the finished product in your hands. I know that man at my book signing was not unusual, that there are countless people just like him: reluctant but potentially great leaders who just need a little help overcoming the hesitation that's holding them back.

When I finally started gathering my thoughts and outlining this book, I realized that I first saw an example of reluctant leadership when I was a boy. My sister, Mary Ellen, was born with Down syndrome in 1947, which was something my parents hadn't given a thought to until my sister arrived. In those days there was very little help for children with intellectual disabilities or their parents. Often the children were warehoused in institutions under deplorable conditions, a situation my parents didn't realize, but which suddenly deeply troubled them. They didn't consider themselves to be leaders and never aspired to pursue or promote a cause, but circumstances seemed to be calling them, so they took a few tentative steps. Before long they were full-blown activists, pressing for political change, organizing fundraising efforts, and doing whatever else they could think of to make people aware of the need for better care and resources for Down syndrome families. Perhaps most importantly they worked tirelessly to improve the conditions in those nightmarish facilities. My father even helped organize a benefit football game, which is still held annually and is sponsored by the Delaware Foundation Reaching Citizens with Intellectual Disabilities.

Many years later I would find myself having a similar experience when I was diagnosed with multiple myeloma, a deadly blood cancer. For fifty years I had been a leader in the world of professional sports. It was my comfort zone, my happy place, and with one sentence out of a doctor's mouth, it was all turned upside down. I knew nothing about multiple myeloma or what to expect from it, and the last thing I wanted to do was put my other plans on hold while I dealt with it.

To say the least, I was reluctant.

> The need for leadership can come calling when you least expect or desire it. It pounds on the door of your existence, shouting its demands and caring nothing about the comfortable circumstances of your well-ordered life.

But as I underwent chemotherapy and stem cell transplant procedures, a whole new world opened up to me: the world of the cancer patient. In no time I was speaking, writing, teaching, and fundraising to cure cancer. It was a role I never asked for and didn't want but couldn't refuse.

These experiences have made it clear to me that the need for leadership can come calling when you least expect or desire it. It pounds on the door of your existence, shouting its demands and caring nothing about the comfortable circumstances of your well-ordered life. Rare is the person who is happy for this moment to come and eager to jump in and lead. The vast majority freeze and say, "Who, me?" My purpose in this book is to take you on a journey from "Who, me?" to "Why not me?"

This journey will unfold as we analyze and answer the nine critical points of reluctance that hesitant leaders inevitably face. We'll do it with truth, common sense, humor, and a host of powerful stories drawn from history and today's fast-paced leadership world. When we reach our destination, not only will the leader inside you be ready to be unleashed, but you will also know how to encourage and motivate others in your organization to overcome their reluctance and start reaching their full leadership potential.

So, buckle up and let's go! This could be one of the most important journeys you'll ever make.

CHAPTER I

Reluctant to Take Charge

Leadership is about moments. Great leaders know the right moment to speak. The right moment to keep quiet. The right moment to change course. The right moment to stay the course. The right moment to challenge. The right moment to console. The right moment to give a pat on the back. The right moment to give a kick in the seat of the pants.

But before all of these moments comes the most important moment of all, the moment that all leadership hinges on. Call it the "take charge moment."

Have you ever been in a situation where there was a job to be done and everyone was talking about it but no one was doing anything? It's often called paralysis by analysis. It's when everyone has an opinion about what should be done, a theory about what might happen if something isn't done, or a fear of what might happen if the wrong thing is done, but no one is doing anything. Opinions and ideas fly like snowflakes in a blizzard while the job sits there waiting to be tackled. Such moments occur all the time in businesses and organizations of every stripe.

Obviously, the answer is for somebody to take charge and get things going. And it sounds so easy. I often hear people say, "If I were running that place, things would sure be different." Or "If I were calling the shots, I'd whip those people into shape." Or "If I were in charge, I wouldn't put up with that." But most of the people who say such things know they're never going to actually be in charge and would go running for the hills if someone ever said to them, "Here, you take over." Taking charge is an easy thing to talk about but a hard thing to do.

Think about Moses.

He is arguably the all-time world champion leader. The guy absolutely reeked of leadership ability. But that "take charge moment" almost finished him before he could get started.

You may remember that God spoke to him out of a burning bush and told him to go to Egypt and confront Pharaoh, the most powerful and ruthless man in the world. Moses was to demand the release of his countrymen, the Jews, from slavery and then oversee their escape from Egypt before leading them on a journey to their new home in the land of Canaan. Moses was thrilled to hear that God was going to liberate his people and would have cheered any man who was put in charge of the project. He just didn't want to be that man.

What I find humorous, and so very telling, is that Moses's primary excuse for not wanting to take charge of this project was his lack of eloquence. But in arguing with God, he demonstrated extraordinary eloquence! He didn't stammer or stutter or fumble his words at all, which just goes to show how intimidating that "take charge moment" can be. We are often willing to demean ourselves, to belittle our gifts, to cast ourselves in an unbecoming light just to avoid it.

Here's something I hope you'll remember: it's always wrong to diminish yourself. It's always wrong to disparage the talents and abilities God has given you. They are precious gifts that should always be valued. If there are legitimate reasons why you can't accept a leadership role, fine. State them and move on. But never try to wiggle out of a call to lead by saying things about yourself that aren't true. To do so is to disrespect yourself and the God who made you.

Back to Moses.

Wearing his reluctance like a cloak, Moses did eventually take charge of the job God had for him to do, though he wasn't crazy about it. I can just imagine the muttering he must have been doing, bending his brother Aaron's ear as they trudged toward Egypt: "I can't believe I'm doing this. I'm a shepherd, for crying out loud! There must be somebody, somewhere who is more qualified for this mission than I am. Why would God pick me?"

But we all know what happened. Over the next several decades, Moses became one of the greatest leaders the world has ever known. Entire books have been written that analyze his leadership style, his courage, and his wisdom. Many experts, even those who are not religious, feel that this man who was once the ultimate reluctant leader is a "must study" for any aspiring young leader today.

Which brings up an important point.

History reveals that a reluctance to take charge is often a key indicator that a leader will do a great job, while an eagerness to take charge is often a sign that a leader will not do a great job. Sounds counterintuitive, I know. And it's

History reveals that a reluctance to take charge is often a key indicator that a leader will do a great job, while an eagerness to take charge is often a sign that a leader will not do a great job.

not always true, hence the use of the word "often." But you might be surprised how often it works out this way.

Let's think about a couple of heads of state, for example.

George Washington is revered as the father of our country, but if you think he was a wily, ambitious politician on a mission to be the first president, you're mistaken. When he returned to Mount Vernon after the Revolutionary War, he was worn and weary, having lost more battles than he had won and witnessed the deaths of countless men. He longed to spend time with Martha and his two stepchildren and decompress from years of hardship. The only reason he went to the Constitutional Convention in 1787 was because James Madison and Henry Knox talked him into it. The notion of being the nation's first president was not a dream that was burning in his heart. At his inauguration he even sounded like a very reluctant leader, talking about the anxiety he felt stepping into such an important position.

Contrast Washington's story to that of Adolf Hitler. Over a decade before Hitler became chancellor of Germany, he was involved in politics and even led an attempted coup in Munich in 1923. The coup failed, and he was put in jail, but that didn't hinder his ambitions. From jail he wrote *Mein Kampf* and further fine-tuned his political goals. When released, he began a campaign to gain a following, often giving vitriolic speeches in beer halls that whipped people into a frenzy. Hitler was a man possessed, driven by his fever-pitched lust to seize and wield power.

Washington and Hitler are representative of the differences we often see when we stand a reluctant leader and an ambitious leader side by side. A few of them are as follows:

Ambitious leaders usually have a personal agenda of self-promotion, while reluctant leaders focus more on just getting the job done.

Ambitious leaders usually have huge egos and illusions of grandeur, while reluctant leaders are well aware of their limitations.

Ambitious leaders usually see gifted people as a threat, while reluctant leaders see gifted people as a much-needed resource.

Ambitious leaders usually surround themselves with "yes men," while reluctant leaders are happy to hear differing points of view that might be helpful.

For these reasons and more, A. W. Tozer said, "I believe that it might be accepted as a fairly reliable rule of thumb that the man who is ambitious to lead is disqualified as a leader."[1] I'm not willing to go quite that far, but history and experience do suggest that it is wise to be at least a bit wary of that person who's chomping at the bit to take charge.

So, this is great news and something you can feel good about. Being reluctant to take charge is not such a bad thing after all! It might even be one of your primary qualifications for being a leader—the fact that you don't see leadership as a way to elevate and glorify yourself but rather as a way to get important things accomplished.

But the reluctance to take charge still needs to be overcome. Let's explore four ways you can do it.

Suggestion #1:
Start Trusting the Opinions of People Who Know You

When I was playing minor league baseball in the Phillies organization, it was becoming increasingly apparent that I was not going to be the next Yogi Berra or Roy Campanella. You've heard of five-tool players (run, field, throw, hit, and hit with power)? Let's just say you could

---

1 A. W. Tozer, "Tozer Devotional: Reluctant Leaders," The Alliance, accessed November 6, 2020, https://www.cmalliance.org/devotions/tozer?id=1296.

multiply my tools by two and still not get to five. But the Phillies saw something else in me that piqued their interest: leadership ability. Instead of giving me a handshake and sending me off to sell insurance, they encouraged me to start learning the business/management side of baseball. There seemed to be a consensus among the higher-ups that I had the tools to excel off the field in ways I would never excel on it.

This is the first key to overcoming your reluctance to lead. If people who understand leadership and know you well believe you have what it takes to succeed in a leadership role, there's every reason to believe they're right.

Consider the fact that they are not going to recruit you to a leadership role if they believe you will hinder the work of their organization. They are not going to want to spend time and effort training you if they think it's all going to be a waste of time. And most of all, unless they are exceedingly cruel, they are not going to want to give you false hope for a future they believe you aren't equipped to achieve.

Your challenge is to trust what they're telling you, which may not be easy if you've had people in your life filling your head with negative thoughts about yourself. For many people, the biggest challenge they face is somehow digging out from underneath the mountain of put-downs and insults that have been heaped upon them. Thoughtless parents can be the worst when it comes to this. You may remember the telephone message the actor Alec Baldwin left for his adolescent daughter in which he called her "a rude, thoughtless little pig."[2] Who *wouldn't* have self-image issues with words like that ringing in his or her ears?

---

2 Carly Mine, "When Alec Baldwin's Voicemail to Daughter Ireland Went Viral," Yahoo!, May 4, 2017, https://www.yahoo.com/entertainment/alec-baldwins-voicemail-daughter-ireland-went-viral-035812127.html.

But it's not just the negative voices in our lives. Culture itself places almost impossible demands on young people especially, suggesting that if they don't look a certain way or dress a certain way or have the right friends or the right sneakers or the right phone, they just don't measure up. And when you've been programmed to believe that you don't measure up, someone coming along and telling you that you have potential can be hard to believe.

My advice in this area is simple: even if you don't believe in yourself, don't begrudge others the privilege of believing in you. If people see something in you that you don't see in yourself, don't automatically brand them as crazy or clueless. Give them a little credit. They are looking at you from a different perspective and may well see what you cannot.

Suggestion #2:
Clarify Your Understanding of the Leadership Task at Hand

It's very common to look at a task and see it as hopelessly huge or complicated or demanding, especially if it's the kind of project you've never tackled before. And the fact that *you're* being asked to lead the effort with so little experience makes you wonder if every other leadership candidate has turned and run for the hills! Well, don't panic. Let me tell you how to shrink any leadership task into three easy steps.

First, clearly define the objective. You'd be surprised how many tasks are undertaken without anyone having pinned down exactly what the goal is. It makes about as much sense as going to the archery range and firing off a quiver full of arrows without setting up the targets first, but it happens more than you might think, and with terrible results.

If you don't clearly define the objective, you have no way of knowing if you're making progress.

Second, take inventory of your human resources. Whom do you have to work with? Is a team already in place? What skills do your team members have relative to the objective? Do you need to recruit more help? The English dramatist John Heywood is credited with the saying, "Many hands make light work." He was right. I've written extensively about the importance of building a team. There are many reasons to do it, but one of the biggest is simply that it whittles a job down to size.

Third, break the project down into its component parts. Most large projects are simply a lot of small projects stuck together. Like a football team is broken down into the offensive, defensive, and special teams units, virtually any leadership project has smaller jobs that can be separated out and handled apart from the whole. Then, as they are accomplished, the project begins to come together and take shape.

Always remember, there is no large leadership challenge that can't be shrunk, thus making even the biggest ones seem less intimidating.

Suggestion #3:

Identify Your Inner Circle of Trusted Associates

Jesus had his disciples.

The president has his cabinet.

The CEO has his board of directors.

The plant manager has his foremen.

The head coach has his assistant coaches.

The pastor has his elders.

You get the idea.

For thousands of years it has been accepted practice for top-level leaders to surround themselves with a capable inner circle that can assist them in getting things done. But for some reason, new, inexperienced, reluctant leaders generally envision themselves flying solo. They imagine themselves getting in over their heads and having nowhere to turn. Such thoughts would make anyone a reluctant leader!

Finding an inner circle of trusted associates to help you carry the burden of responsibility is one of the biggest steps you as a new leader can take toward success. But it must be done carefully. Here are some guidelines that will help you choose the right people.

First, look for people of integrity. It's been said, and it's true, that who you are is much more important than what you do, making integrity the leadership trait that towers above all others. You must have it to be successful, and so must your inner circle. You need people around you who will be honest and tell you the truth rather than just telling you what they think you want to hear. You need people around you who are not two-faced, supporting you to your face and undermining you behind your back. And if something goes wrong, you need people around you who will be honest about what happened and not try to cover it up. History is filled with examples of leaders who were undermined, and in some cases destroyed, because someone in the inner circle lacked integrity.

Second, look for people who are loyal and happy serving in a supporting role. Nothing ignites conflict quicker than a close subordinate who pretends to be supportive but secretly wants to be in charge. In the Bible a man named Korah decided he could do a better job than Moses and started badmouthing him at every turn, gathering other malcontents around his opinion that Moses needed to be replaced. Trouble started to brew, and before the dust settled over fourteen thousand people had died. You probably won't see people die if someone is jealous of you and trying to usurp your authority, but the project you're trying to get done just might. And that's not to mention how miserable you will be as you try to cope with the badmouthing and backstabbing of people who are supposed to be helping you.

Third, look for people who are strong where you are weak. The United States has had presidents who were military men, such as General Dwight D. Eisenhower. A man of his experience would obviously be well versed in military matters and national defense but could not be expected to have the same grasp of domestic matters such as housing and urban development. Imagine how counterproductive it would be for such a president to load his cabinet with all his military buddies and choose no one who was savvy with domestic concerns.

Early in my leadership journey, I discovered the importance of having a great personal assistant who could handle all the administrative details that would certainly overwhelm me if I had to deal with them. Anyone who knows me will tell you that I am not Mr. Technology. People around me were on their fourth or fifth iPhone when I was still sending smoke signals! But all is well because I have people in my life who are strong where I am weak.

Fourth, look for people who have thick skin. There will come a day when a member of your inner circle will passionately advise you to do something that you don't think is best. When you say, "No, we're going to go in a different direction," what will he or she do? Pout? Sulk? Grumble to other members of the team? This is a critical question. You can't afford to have your leadership compromised by the constant need to coddle the people in your inner circle. You must develop a culture where everyone can speak honestly and respectfully without the fear of hurt feelings.

Fifth, look for people with endurance who will stick with you over the long haul. Many are the leadership projects that run into complications, get bogged down, or encounter delays. Often the problems will have nothing to do with your leadership choices. Building projects, for example, can run into problems with inspectors, subcontractors, codes, and suppliers. When things don't go as planned, you need people who are going to hang in there. It's never ideal when you have to seek out new blood in the middle of a project because someone you were counting on got frustrated and quit.

Bottom line: don't think you have to be the Lone Ranger. Build your inner circle and let them help you succeed.

Suggestion #4:

Don't Take Your Leadership Task Too Seriously

As counterintuitive as it seems at first glance, I must close with this word of advice, because if you're a reluctant leader taking charge of a project for the first time in your life, you will no doubt see it as a momentous thing. It is, of course, in one way. It marks a new chapter in your life and possibly the beginning of a lifelong leadership adventure. But you must not give it too much weight in your thinking. What do I mean? Three things.

First, don't let the project define you. The project, whatever it may be, is likely temporary and will be over and done with and forgotten about at some point, while your life will go on. If you want to be defined by something, be defined by good character, by the way you treat your spouse and children, by the grace and kindness you show to others, or by your faith in God. These are not temporary projects but daily disciplines. They are the things that really matter.

Dean Smith, the legendary basketball coach at the University of North Carolina who won two NCAA national championships, once said that you should never put too much emphasis on one game. He pointed out that if you live and die with every game, you will be dead a lot. This advice applies to leadership projects as well. They will come and go. Some may turn out good, and some may turn out bad. Don't let something so temporary define you.

Second, don't let the project deflate you. Don't grant the project so much importance that it deflates your spirit if it doesn't go well. Understand that leadership failures happen all the time and are often not wholly the fault of the leader.

Baseball Hall of Famer Joe Torre knows this very well. His first three managerial assignments were with the Mets, Braves, and Cardinals. They didn't go well. But Joe understood that in each case a primary factor was that he didn't have enough good players. He said, "I never fell for the illusion that I'd done a perfect job. Nor did I blame others. I simply made a realistic assessment of my situation and concluded that it wasn't all my fault. I refused to write myself off as a major league manager with the potential to win a world championship."[3] Joe ended up winning six American League Pennants and four World Series with the Yankees.

That's exactly what I'm talking about. I hate to think how many truly great leaders there are whose talent the world would have been deprived of if they had allowed their initial failed attempts at leadership to crush their spirit and convince them to give up the thought of ever trying again. If you study leadership like I have, you know that a failed attempt at leadership is a virtual prerequisite for leadership success. Almost nobody hits a home run his first time at bat. So, instead of slinking away to hide in the shadows after an unspectacular first try at leadership, be eager for a new opportunity, realizing that you are now smarter than you were before.

Almost nobody hits a home run his first time at bat.

3 Joe Torre, *Ground Rules for Winners* (New York: Hyperion, 1999), 9.

Third, don't let the project demean you. Many a new leader has taken charge of a project and discovered that a little dishonesty here or a little bending of the rules there is par for the course among those who are more experienced. "It's the way the world works," they'll say. "You can't beat the system," they'll say. "Just roll with it," they'll say. And shortcuts and shady moves might seem like a good way to get ahead. But when you demean yourself in the interest of success, you have lost, no matter how well the project turns out in the end.

As of this writing, the Houston Astros are being investigated for electronically stealing signs at their home ballpark. According to reports, the Astros used an outfield camera to relay signs to a computer workstation that was set up in the tunnel that leads from the dugout to the clubhouse. From there, someone would bang on a garbage can with a baseball bat to send a message to the hitter. This story would be cringeworthy under any circumstances, but it's even more so because the sign-stealing took place during the 2017 season, the year the Astros won the World Series.

It remains to be seen what the investigation will reveal or what the fallout will be. But the accusation, made by a member of the 2017 Astros team, begs a few questions. What success is worth the sacrifice of your character? What victory is truly a victory if you have to demean yourself in order to gain it? Even if you hold a trophy, are you really a champion if you have to cheat in order to win? In my view—and in the view of anybody with integrity—it's better to lose or to quit and walk away than to diminish yourself morally and spiritually. Take your leadership task seriously, but not so seriously that you are willing to demean yourself in order to succeed.

No American who's old enough to remember September 11, 2001, will ever forget the gut-wrenching images of planes crashing into buildings, billowing plumes of smoke, and terrified citizens running for their lives in the streets of New York City. But out of that horror came stories of heroism that are unsurpassed in American history. One happened aboard United Airlines flight 93, bound from New Jersey to San Francisco.

At 9:30 a.m., about fifty minutes into the flight, three men charged the cockpit. Air traffic controllers in Cleveland heard enough over an open mic to know that the plane was being hijacked. The voices of the hijackers, along with wails and screams and pleas not to be hurt, left no doubt that the unthinkable was happening. Suddenly the plane began to turn toward Washington, DC.

As it tore through the sky, a flurry of calls was being made by the passengers. They realized that their lives were likely coming to an end and began trying to reach their loved ones. Todd Beamer's call reached an air phone operator named Lisa Jefferson. They spoke briefly. He asked her to contact his wife and tell her he loved her. Then, with the connection still open, she heard him plotting with others to jump the hijackers. Though much of the conversation was unintelligible, Ms. Jefferson distinctly heard Todd Beamer say, "You ready? Okay, let's roll."

There are no living witnesses to what happened next. The cockpit recorder did pick up the sounds of a fight with screams and crashes. More importantly, the plane began to descend, eventually crashing in a field in rural Pennsylvania. It is not known where the hijackers were hoping to crash the plane. Most believe it was the US Capitol or the White House. Suffice to say, many people who might have died that day were spared because of the actions of a handful of brave souls.

I often think about Todd Beamer's words, "Okay, let's roll." They are the words of a reluctant but amazing leader. When he boarded the plane that day, leading a violent attack against terrorists was the furthest thing from his mind. As a seller of database software for the

Oracle Corporation, it was not something he was prepared for. But in the moment, someone needed to take charge, and he did.

Though perhaps in not such an important or dramatic or urgent way, there's every reason to believe that life will someday thrust you into a situation where leadership is needed. When that time comes, there will certainly be excuses you can make. There will likely be others you can point to who might be more qualified. Just remember this: nothing good can happen until somebody takes charge. Reluctant though you may be, I hope you'll be willing to step forward when others are stepping back.

CHAPTER 2

Reluctant to Delegate

Entertainment has grown a little strange in recent years. Season ten of *America's Got Talent* featured Stevie Starr, a fifty-six-year-old professional regurgitator.

Yes, you read that right. A professional regurgitator.

You've heard the old saying, "What goes up must come down." Well, in Mr. Starr's case, what goes down will most assuredly come up, if and when he wants it to. I'm talking about all kinds of things, from light bulbs to car keys to goldfish. He says he developed the ability to throw up on cue when he was a kid living in an orphanage. Apparently, swallowing his money was the only way he could keep it from being stolen. Later, if he wanted an ice cream cone, well, you get the idea. If you're thinking that the *AGT* judges were grossed out and sent Mr. Starr packing, think again. They loved him as he barfed his way to a fourth-place finish.

Yes, entertainment has changed a lot. In my day a juggler riding a unicycle was a crowd-pleaser. Or the plate spinner. Remember the plate spinner?

He had a long table with about ten flimsy rods sticking up from it that were evenly spaced. At one end of the table he had a stack of glass dinner plates, one of which he would smash on the floor to prove they were real. Then, to the accompaniment of music, he would start the plates spinning on the rods, one at a time, working his way down the table. The first four or five were no problem. But as he progressed, the first plates he had set in motion would start slowing down and wobbling, requiring him to run back and speed them up, then dash back to where he had left off and start more plates spinning. The idea was to get plates spinning on all ten rods at once. The drama was in the spinner's constant running back and forth, trying to keep the plates going so that none of them crashed to the floor. It wasn't high-tech, but it was frantic and fun.

I've often thought that the plate spinner's act perfectly depicts what a lot of leaders go through when they tackle a big job. They find themselves dashing here and there, scrambling frantically to try to start and keep all the project's plates spinning. The difference being that an entertainer who spins plates gets to stop after a few minutes and soak up the applause of the audience, while the leader who's trying to handle every detail of a leadership project all by himself has to struggle on and on, often with no end in sight. Inevitably, frustration and fatigue set in and the plates start getting more and more wobbly, often resulting in an epic crash.

This is why delegation is a leader's best friend.

Delegation would entail the leader assembling a team of capable plate spinners and assigning only a plate or two to each one. The spinners would see to their assigned plates, keeping them spinning with barely a wobble and a minimum of stress, while the leader tends to other matters.

J. C. Penney, one of history's most successful businessmen, was a strong proponent of delegation. He started working at a dry goods store in 1902, almost a full century before Amazon was launched. He was young but had a good head for business. So good that within eight years he owned thirteen stores of his own. By 1917 he owned 175 stores. He is credited with inventing the concept of franchising and pioneering the practice of storing goods in regional warehouses so they could be shipped more quickly and at a lower cost. It is not inaccurate to say that J. C. Penney was the Jeff Bezos of his time.

As his business exploded, J. C. Penney said, "I have found my most successful associates by giving men responsibility, by making them feel that I relied upon them; and those who have proved to be unworthy have only caused the others, who far outnumbered them, to stand in a clearer light. This principle, at least in measure, is responsible for the success of our mercantile operation."[4]

I was never in the mercantile business, but in my life as a sports executive, I quickly learned the value of delegation. My first official leadership job was running a minor league ball club for the Philadelphia Phillies organization. You name it, I was responsible for it. I had to make sure the field was ready to play on, the concessions were fit to eat, and the national anthem singer was hired and had a working microphone. I had to see to it that the litter was picked up, the trash emptied, and the restrooms cleaned after every game. I had to plan the promotions we used to draw fans to the ballpark. I had to make sure the tickets were printed and that there were enough people to sell the tickets at the windows and tear them in two at the turnstiles. And of course, there were ushers needed in every section of the ballpark

---

4 Peter Krass, *The Little Book of Business Wisdom* (New York: Wiley & Sons, 2001), 45.

to direct people to their seats. I had to hire them and train them and make sure they all had matching shirts.

I learned very quickly that my survival would depend on my ability to delegate. It is no exaggeration to say that delegating these various jobs to capable, well-trained people prevented me from being an abject failure. And delegation has continued to serve me well over the years. I concur with Teddy Roosevelt, who said, "The best executive is the one who has sense enough to pick good men to do what he wants done, and self-restraint enough to keep from meddling with them while they do it."[5]

All of this seems so obvious, I know. But you'd be surprised how many leaders are reluctant to delegate. Let me run down a few reasons why.

First, there is the notion many leaders have that nobody can do the job as well as they can. Often this is true. When I was the general manager of the 76ers, we created a new mascot but had a terrible time finding someone to put the suit on and make the character come to life in the way I envisioned. Finally, in a moment of complete frustration, I decided to put the suit on myself. For one game I was "Hoops," dancing, cavorting, and generally getting into all sorts of shenanigans on the sidelines and in the stands. At one point I even stuck my head into our opponent's huddle during a time out and was shoved out of the way by the team's coach, who happened to be a longtime friend of mine: Seattle's Lenny Wilkens. I know he thought there was some clueless kid in the suit, and I never told him otherwise. He was irritated for sure, but the fans loved it!

---

5 Norbert Juma, "65 Theodore Roosevelt Quotes About Leadership and Success," Everyday Power, November 14, 2019. https://everydaypower.com/theodore-roosevelt-quotes/.

Yes, you may be able to do the job better than anyone else. That isn't the point. The point is that you will die if you try to do everything. Find people who have ability and are willing to try. Train them well, and let them grow into the job. People almost always get better at what they do as time goes on.

Second, many leaders are reluctant to delegate because of the extra time it takes to recruit and train new people. Ironically, many of those leaders who think they don't have time to recruit and train people will be the first ones to complain about being overworked! It makes no sense to disdain the one thing (delegation) that will solve your most frustrating problem (being overworked), but leaders do it all the time. It's like having a toothache and telling yourself you don't have time to go to the dentist.

While it's true that recruiting and training people is a time- and energy-consuming endeavor up front, you do eventually get past that stage and begin to reap the benefits, such as more rest, less stress, or even the freedom to pursue new challenges. Few things you ever do as a leader will pay off as much as recruiting and training people to help you carry the load.

Few things you ever do as a leader will pay off as much as recruiting and training people to help you carry the load.

Third, insecure leaders are reluctant to delegate because they are afraid their newly empowered subordinates will begin to overshadow them. Many leaders get their self-esteem from their work. In my experience, this is especially true of men. I've been around many strong male leaders my whole life, and I've seen it again and again—when two alpha males are introduced, the first question they ask of each other is, "What do you do?" In other words, "Your name isn't important. I just want to know how I compare to you career-wise." It's as if they are instantly measuring themselves by each other's accomplishments.

So, imagine this kind of insecure leader contemplating delegation. It will be very easy for him or her to conjure up images of the new recruit excelling at the job, getting attention, gaining a following, earning a promotion, and eventually overshadowing or even replacing him. Suddenly, delegation doesn't sound like such a good idea.

Fourth would be the opposite reason—*some leaders are afraid their newly empowered subordinates will fail and leave them with a mess to clean up.* This is a common fear when delegating to someone who is unproven. Is the person really up to the task? Am I going to look like a fool for choosing him? Will she end up making my job harder instead of easier?

Fifth, some leaders are reluctant to delegate because they hate change. There is a degree to which every person hates change. I, for example, am a big believer in change, but when my wife, Ruth, told me it was time to have a funeral for my old flip phone and get a hot new iPhone, I resisted with all the energy I could muster. Futilely, it turned out, but I did my best, which only goes to show that even people who love change will hate it if it intrudes on their comfort zone. Mark Twain was right when he said, "No one likes change except a wet baby."

I should add that an aversion to change is especially common in churches and other religious organizations. Maybe it's because they are steeped in truths and traditions that are thousands of years old, but churches are notorious for clinging to bygone notions and obsolete methods, which reminds me of an old joke: How many church members does it take to change a light bulb? The answer is seven. One to hold the ladder, one to change the bulb, and five to stand around and talk about how much they're going to miss the old bulb.

Sixth, there are leaders who are reluctant to delegate because they are afraid it might make them look lazy. They imagine a critic confronting them: "What are you trying to do, get other people to do your job?" This is a powerful fear because no one wants to be known as a slacker. In fact, I'm confident that a lot of workaholism is rooted in a passionate and sometimes neurotic need to be perceived as pulling one's own weight. Ironically, people who are obsessed with pulling their own weight are often actually pulling two or three times their own weight because they won't delegate!

Seventh—and I hate to say this—there are too many leaders who are reluctant to delegate because they simply don't want to share the glory for a successful venture. I am always amused when there is a high-profile press conference, perhaps something having to do with law enforcement or maybe a congressional hearing. Whoever is standing at the microphone will be surrounded by a host of associates and dignitaries. They will be surrounding the speaker like a choir ready to burst forth into song, not because they need to be there—not even because they had anything to do with the matter at hand—but because they want to be seen. Elected officials, especially, are famous for wanting to take credit for everything. They can't stand the thought of delegating a job that might have some future glory attached to it.

Yes, there are many reasons why leaders are reluctant to delegate. If you're feeling that reluctance right now, maybe for some combination of the reasons above, let me try to help you break out of it.

The Right Reason to Delegate

This is where all great endeavors begin. You must have a reason for doing it. A reason that makes sense. A reason you can get excited about. So what is the right reason to delegate?

It's not so you can have more free time.

It's not so you can get rid of all the jobs you hate.

It's not so you can gain favor with your employees.

The right reason to delegate is to make things better.

In 1949 bandleader Lawrence Welk, who was himself an accordion player, hired Myron Floren, perhaps the greatest accordion player in the world, to play in his band. But he did it without first consulting his business manager. When his business manager heard about the move, he blew up. "What were you thinking, Lawrence? It's insane to put an accordion player on stage with you who's better than you are. Would Tommy Dorsey hire a trombonist who is better than him? Would Benny Goodman hire a better clarinetist?"

If you're old enough to remember the *Lawrence Welk Show* on TV (or have seen the reruns on PBS), you probably recall Lawrence bouncing his baton up and down while Myron Floren dazzled the audience with his solos. Lawrence was grinning ear to ear (and laughing all the way to the bank) because he knew that Myron Floren elevated his orchestra to a whole new level and was a star that people clamored to see.

The reason to delegate is to make things better.

In the Book of Acts, the church was in its infancy, but already a problem had arisen. Some widows were being neglected in the daily distribution of food. As a result, people were griping. Not just the widows whose stomachs were growling but also their family members. You would gripe too if you felt your granny wasn't being treated properly.

So, the apostles, who were running things, called a meeting. The essential question they addressed was, "How can we make things better?" What they did *not* do was restructure their schedules and try to work in more time to run the food program. What they *did* do was select seven trustworthy men to take over the food program. They delegated because they knew it would make things better.

Your job as a leader is to ask one question over and over again: How can we make things better? Over time different conditions and challenges may produce different answers, but often the answer will be "delegate."

If a task needs more attention than you're able to give it, delegate.

If you want to improve the culture and morale of your team, delegate.

If you want to expand beyond what you're currently doing, delegate.

If you have people on your team whose talents aren't being maximized, delegate.

If you want to tighten up your procedures and make things more efficient, delegate.

If you want to raise up new leaders who will be able to lead into the future, delegate.

But of course you can't delegate recklessly or thoughtlessly. To do so would be to create more problems than you already have. Delegation must be done right.

The Right Way to Delegate

Hitting major league pitching is one of the hardest things in the world to do, but there are lots of ways to do it. In one baseball game you are likely to see every kind of batting stance imaginable. The closed stance and the open stance. The high leg kick and the toe-tap. High hands and low hands. The bat waggle and the still-as-a-statue pose. Rod Carew held the bat so loosely it looked like he might drop it, while Mark McGwire looked like he might squeeze the bat handle into sawdust.

Most of life's endeavors offer multiple ways to be successful. Not so with delegation. That's because delegating isn't an art, it's a science, which means the proper elements have to be there to get the desired results. The list of guidelines that follow are time-tested and well proven. Taken together, they are the perfect recipe for delegating effectively. Ignore them at your peril!

First, make sure you delegate to people with whom you get along well. Some leaders unwisely use delegation as a tool to try to improve a shaky relationship. They think, "Maybe if I give him an important job, it will improve his attitude toward me." It might, of course. But the job could just as easily become a knife with which that person who doesn't like you can stab you in the back. You will be wise to elevate no one in your organization that hasn't proven him or herself to be a team player.

This does not mean, however, that you should delegate to "yes people." Former University of Tennessee women's basketball coach Pat Summit, one of the most successful basketball coaches in history, always said that she wanted people on her staff who would think for themselves and challenge her decisions. She said she knew she would never get better if no one ever forced her to consider ideas that stretched beyond her own impulses. So, pick people you relate well to, people who are supportive, but not people who are afraid to speak their mind if they happen to have a better idea.

Second, delegate those things you're not very good at, and keep doing the things that are in your wheelhouse. One of the biggest reasons why churches have grown so large in recent years is because preachers finally started understanding what they were doing wrong. Instead of focusing on preaching and vision-casting and letting other talented people run the church, they were trying to preach and cast vision *and* manage every little detail of church life, from lawn maintenance to ushering schedules. In many cases, this was the model they had grown up with in the church they attended, or how they were taught in college. Once they figured out what an advantage it was to focus on what they're good at and let others take care of everything else, it was like the lid blew off. Suddenly churches were doubling and tripling in size. We no longer even raise our eyebrows when we think of a church running ten thousand members or more.

Remember that delegation is not just about lightening your load, it's about making things better. There are leaders who don't even use the word "delegate." They prefer to call it "upgrading." Your ultimate goal should be to have everyone on the team doing what they're good at and no one doing what they're not good at.

Third, make sure the person you're delegating work to understands why his or her job is important. Right now, there are millions of people who have no enthusiasm for their work. They slog through the motions, day after day, half performing their duties, not just because they don't like what they do but often because they don't see the point of what they do. You should be able to look every person on your team in the eye and say, "Here's why your job is important." If you can't do that, then maybe that job should be eliminated!

Think carefully about this.

Many projects and programs and ideas are allowed to outlive their usefulness. They serve a useful purpose in the beginning, but over time, as needs change, they become more about keeping a tradition alive than actually contributing to the success of the organization. This is especially true in older organizations. Wise is the leader who before delegating the job asks the hard question, "Do we even need to be doing this anymore?"

Fourth, don't just delegate work, delegate authority. As a parent, you give your kids chores to do. You tell them to take out the trash or mow the grass or wash the car. They're jobs and nothing more. You don't empower them with authority because they are children and their judgment can't be trusted. Always remember that your teammates are not children. They are adults who have fully formed brains, who can think through problems and find solutions—if you will let them. Obviously, you must give them a framework within which to operate. Lay out parameters and ask them to operate within them. If you do this, you will be helping to create a leader, not just employing the services of an automaton.

Further, by delegating authority as well as work, you eliminate the frustration of having people constantly running back to you with every little problem or question. Many workers know exactly what needs to be done to solve a problem—they even know before they ask what their boss is going to say … but are still expected to ask because of the boss's insecurity. What a waste of time and energy! Let your people make decisions.

Fifth, resist the temptation to micromanage people, but establish a system by which everyone can be held accountable. If you've ever had a boss looking over your shoulder and watching your every move, you know how debilitating it is. In workplaces where people are micromanaged, morale is almost always low and employee turnover high because people get tired of the constant meddling and the lack of trust. Talk to people who've worked for a micromanager and you'll hear lots of complaining coupled with expressions of joy that they were able to escape.

The other big problem with micromanaging is that it builds a culture of dependency. When people become used to being micromanaged, they grow fearful of handling problems and making decisions on their own. The kind of spirited, "go get 'em" attitude that makes an employee truly great is almost completely squelched.

At the same time, people don't want to feel like the boss has stuck them with a job and then gone off and forgotten about them. The key is to strike a happy medium. Let your people work freely without you constantly badgering them, but establish a plan whereby they will periodically have to present, explain, and, if need be, defend their work.

Sixth, acknowledge your people's successes. In 1968 Ohio State University started the practice of giving their football players helmet stickers to acknowledge in-game achievements. They had no idea the players would respond so well and become so determined to meet the high standards that would earn them a sticker. Suddenly, as the helmets started filling up with stickers, the team was playing better and winning more games. When word got around, other schools were jumping in and printing up their own helmet stickers. Lots of teams use them today.

There's an old saying that if you acknowledge something good that happens, you increase the chance of it happening again. Apple, perhaps the most successful company in the world, understands this, which is why they celebrate everything from R&D breakthroughs to product milestones to sales increases to new product lines to hot new apps to new hires. And since they don't wear helmets, they do it with commemorative T-shirts. Some Apple employees have hundreds of T-shirts, and there's even a coffee table book that is nothing but pictures of those celebratory shirts. You will never go wrong by patting people on the back and acknowledging their good work.

Before I wrap up this chapter, I want to talk about something that often happens when work is delegated. It's called *reverse delegation*, and it's not a good thing.

Imagine that you have delegated a job to someone in your organization. Three weeks later the person comes back to you and says, "I've got a problem with this" and lays it out for you. Because you are a good person and care about your employee, you say, "Hmm, let me think about it and get back to you."

Do you realize what just happened?

The job was just delegated back to you … or reverse delegated.

Always remember that the person who determines the next step for the project owns the project. If the problem is on your desk, if people are waiting for you to find an answer, make a decision, or handle a problem, *you* are the owner of that project. Forget any delegation you may think you have done. That puppy has landed right back in your lap. It's as if you never delegated it in the first place.

Which means as a leader you can't let yourself fall into the trap of being too nice. It seems cold to look at your employee who's coming to you with a problem and say, "I gave that job to you. I need for you to figure out a solution and make it happen." But if you don't do this, the jobs you delegate will keep coming back to you just as surely as the swallows return to Capistrano.

As with any problem, an ounce of prevention is worth a pound of cure, and that is certainly true of reverse delegation. You can largely prevent it by choosing wisely whom you delegate to, by giving adequate training, and by empowering your people to make decisions and find solutions from the get-go. Will they occasionally make a less than perfect decision? Certainly. But that is not the end of the world. A bad decision can be very instructive. It can lead to a better choice down the road. If you're scared of a bad decision being made, you shouldn't be in leadership in the first place.

One day President Dwight D. Eisenhower was signing letters that were to be mailed. An aide who would be taking the letters away to the mail room stood by, watching. Letter after letter was signed and stacked. Finally the aide said, "Mr. President, I don't know how you have time to write all these letters and still focus on the business of the country."

The president laughed and said, "Son, I didn't write any of these letters. I haven't even read them. But I know the people who did write them, and I trust those people."

Don't be reluctant to delegate. Done right, it will launch you to a whole new level of effectiveness.

CHAPTER 3

Reluctant to Take Risks

Imagine that you're broke. You have a baby on the way and not enough money to pay the bills. You decide to try something that might make you a big chunk of money, such as writing a screenplay for a Hollywood movie. You've never done it before and you know it's a long shot, but you've got a cool idea and some writing skills and you believe you can do it. And besides, you don't have any other bright ideas. So you sit down and go to work.

Four days later you put a period at the end of the last sentence and sit back in your chair. Your gut tells you that what you've just written is pretty good, but doesn't everybody love their own writing? Only one way to find out. So out the door you go, shopping your work to people who make movies.

It goes well. Really well. You are delighted to find a studio that wants to buy your script. You're even more delighted when you find out that studio is willing to pay big money for it. *Big* money. The kind of money that will solve all your financial problems, and then some. So what do you do?

You turn down the offer and walk away.

Right now, you're thinking the above story went from far-fetched to ridiculous. Such a thing would never happen. Nobody who's broke would ever turn down a huge advance for something he'd written. The story has to be a fairy tale.

No, it isn't. It actually happened.

The broke scriptwriter was Sylvester Stallone. The script he wrote was for a little movie called *Rocky*. You're thinking, "But wait a minute, Pat. That movie *was* made. It was very popular. It won an Academy Award. Everybody loves it!"

Yes, yes, yes, and yes.

But Stallone did not accept the first offer. He tucked his script under his arm and walked out the door because he had his heart set on playing the part of Rocky and the studio made it clear that it wanted to find its own actor.

What a risk!

He left more money than he'd ever seen before on the table and walked out the door with no guarantee that another offer would come along. But come along it did, and the rest is pop culture history. The movie was made, and Stallone played Rocky, paid his bills, and became a Hollywood icon. The Rocky statue that stands outside the Philadelphia Museum of Art is the ultimate monument, not just to a beloved movie character but also to the importance of risk-taking.

I can't think of a single significant accomplishment or advancement in the human race that was accomplished without someone taking a risk. Think about the last time you ate an egg. As you were wolfing it down, did you stop to think about the first person who ever ate an egg? Imagine that moment. Said person sees something drop out of a chicken's posterior and thinks, "Hmm, I wonder what would happen if I ate that?"

Or what about the first person who ate a raw oyster?

It sounds like a joke, but I'm serious.

Even the simplest advancements in history, such as figuring out what's safe to eat, involved risk. Then you can think about the explorers who left homes and families to blaze trails through unknown lands. Think about Christopher Columbus and the Pilgrims and our founding fathers. Think about the Wright Brothers and Charles Lindbergh and Neil Armstrong. Think about Churchill and Roosevelt during World War II. We might all be speaking German today without their risky moves.

But the ultimate in risky moves comes to us from the Spanish-American War. American doctors were studying yellow fever, trying to figure out how it was passed from one person to another. They had guesses but no scientific evidence, so they decided on a course of action that was about as risky as you can get.

First, they took some mosquitos and fed them on some yellow fever patients. Then they released those mosquitos into a container of guinea pigs. The guinea pigs got the fever, which proved that mosquitos could give the fever to guinea pigs but didn't prove they could give it to humans. So they ran the experiment again, this time putting themselves in the place of the guinea pigs. The mosquitos dined on them and, yes, they got the fever. One of them even died.

But that's not the end of the story. One more question remained: Could yellow fever be transmitted by touching things that yellow fever patients have touched?

To answer this question, some more of those American doctors went into a home where yellow fever patients had stayed, put on the dirty clothes they had worn, and slept in their beds. They did not get yellow fever. And with the information gained by these amazingly courageous doctors, we were well on our way to conquering a disease that had killed people all over the world.[6]

But it's not just the life-and-death risks of history we should note. Every single day people take risks you won't hear about on the news but that are, for them, monumental.

Every dreamer who starts a business is taking a risk. Every church that hires a new pastor is taking a risk. Every patient who agrees to undergo surgery is taking a risk. Every couple that decides to get married is taking a risk. Every business owner who hires a new employee is taking a risk. And as one who lives in Orlando, which owns some of the most congested roadways in the world and sees about three thousand accidents a year, I can tell you that every person who goes to the grocery store (or anywhere else) is taking a risk!

Risk-taking is so woven into the fabric of our lives that it's almost impossible to get through a day without taking a few. That being the case, you'd think we would be comfortable with the idea. Especially leaders. Surely, any person who has enough skill and intelligence to be handed a leadership position will be an old pro at taking risks, right?

Wrong!

Many people who have taken countless risks throughout their lives suddenly become risk-averse when they are handed the reins of leadership. There are several reasons why this happens.

First, many new leaders when hired or promoted are told in no uncertain terms not to rock the boat. You see this a lot in churches. A new pastor is hired and told right away by his new bosses what the church likes and doesn't like, the implication being that he is not to mess with it. "You can do anything you want as long as you don't mess up the good thing we've got going here" is a common refrain. Often,

---

6 Carl S. Patton, *More Two-Minute Stories* (New York: Willett, Clark & Company, 1937), 17.

the "good thing" they're referring to may not be all that good, but it's comfortable. It's what they're used to and what makes them happy. Mess with it and pay the price.

I love a cartoon that appeared in a Christian magazine a few years ago. It showed two pastors comparing scars on their bodies. One of them had his pants leg pulled up, was pointing to a nasty scar, and saying, "I got this one the first time we used drums in the Sunday morning service." Yes, indeed, the world is full of comfortable people who do not want you to rock their boat.

Second, some new leaders are reluctant to take risks because they've seen others take them and pay a terrible price. On July 31, 2018, the Pittsburgh Pirates traded away two young prospects for an established Major League hurler. They got Chris Archer, a two-time all-star who had led the Tampa Bay Rays organization in just about every pitching category, in the deal, but it was still a risk because the two young players they gave up, outfielder Austin Meadows and pitcher Tyler Glasnow, were highly rated prospects. A year and a half later, as I write these words, that trade looks like a disaster for the Pirates. Meadows and Glasnow have flourished, while Archer has been a shadow of his former self, losing far more games than he's won. How many general managers for other teams have thought about that trade and felt uneasy about trading their own prospects? Probably all of them!

Other people's misfortune always affects us. Have you ever been driving down the highway and passed a serious car wreck, complete with smoke and twisted metal and bodies on stretchers? Makes you slow down, doesn't it? Makes you think twice before you pull that aggressive lane-changing move you might ordinarily go for without thinking. The same is true in leadership. Nobody wants to follow in the footsteps of a person who just walked off a cliff.

Third, some leaders are reluctant to take risks because their definition of success doesn't allow for risks. Not everyone defines success in terms of more and bigger. Some people define success in terms of stability and consistency. If they can get through a year without anything bad happening in their business or organization, they count it a success. Of course, it's very likely that nothing very great will have happened either, but if their definition of success doesn't count that as a negative, they are perfectly happy.

It can be said that many people with such a narrow view of success don't know what they're missing. They might well love what a few well-thought-out risks would bring them in terms of growth and profits, but they haven't stretched their minds far enough to encompass such possibilities. They are the people who respond to suggestions by saying, "It's okay. We're happy with things the way they are."

Fourth, some leaders are reluctant to take risks because of how they were raised. They say that the kind of person you're going to be is pretty much established by the time you're five years old. This makes sense because you learn more in the first five years of life than you do in all the subsequent years of your life combined. And sometimes, depending on your upbringing, what you learn is to play it safe. Many are the overprotective parents who shield their children from any activity that might have some risk attached to it.

At a local Little League game, a batter got plunked on the shoulder by a wild pitch. The ball probably wasn't going faster than forty miles an hour, but when you're eleven, I guess that feels pretty fast. The boy, who was given to theatrics, fell to the ground and screamed like he was having an amputation without anesthesia. His mother, who had apparently never considered the possibility of her son being hit by a pitch, marched onto the field, grabbed him by the wrist, and marched him to the car. The boy never played another game. His mother told her son and everyone else that sports were just too dangerous.

It doesn't take much of an imagination to picture that boy years later in some kind of leadership position where he's having to weigh the pros and cons of a risky venture. I'd say chances are pretty good that he'll be inclined toward the safer path. He may even hear his mother's voice echoing in his mind: "It's just too dangerous!"

Finally, some leaders are reluctant to take risks because they lack confidence in their abilities. They know that if a risk is successful, it could bring dramatic change to the company or organization, change that could potentially extend beyond their giftedness.

I've worked with countless leaders, and I know that most of them have a sense of their capabilities. Life has a way of teaching us what we're good at and not good at. A pastor, for example, who does a great job with a church of 150 people may know that he's not cut out to lead a megachurch. A good high school basketball coach may know that he's not cut out to handle a college program where there are infinitely more rules and much greater demands on the coach and his family. There's certainly nothing wrong with this. In fact, it's very wise to own up to your limitations. Countless leaders have gotten themselves into trouble by biting off more than they could chew. So a leader who feels he's reached the level of responsibility he's best suited for will likely be very reluctant to take risks, even if everyone around him is encouraging him to step out and do something bold.

Let me be clear. Risk-averse leaders may be very good leaders in numerous ways. They may possess great character, be good managers of people, have a gift for conflict resolution, and other considerable abilities. But his reluctance to take risks will always guarantee that his organization has a low ceiling. Former President Jimmy Carter once observed that you have to go out on a limb if you want to find the fruit.

But you shouldn't do it recklessly. Risk-taking is not synonymous with being dumb. Let me give you seven guidelines that will help you be a smart risk-taker.

Guideline #1:

Don't Make a Decision until You've Explored All the Options

While I am all in favor of taking risks, I am not in favor of taking a risk when there is a nonrisky alternative that will accomplish the same thing. No one in his right mind would be in favor of such a thing.

Every off-season, baseball teams, especially the ones that didn't do so well the year before, are under a lot of pressure to make the big free-agent acquisition. There always seems to be one superstar who's played out his contract and is on the auction block, putting fans in a frenzy. But now that it's common for contracts to reach the $30 million range, any such signing is a risk. What if the player gets hurt or doesn't perform up to expectations? In 2019 the Yankees paid Giancarlo Stanton, one of their big free-agent signings, $25 million while he played only eighteen games and hit three home runs.

A wise general manager will scrutinize both his big-league roster and his minor league rosters and see if he has an up-and-coming talent that might be a better—and more reasonable—investment in the long run. He could also explore the trade market. He might even choose to stand pat if he thinks he's got the talent to compete. The big risky signing will get all the headlines on ESPN and make the fans delirious, but the quieter, more conservative move might be the best one for the team. I can assure you from years of experience with these things that your best move will sometimes be the one you *don't* make.

Guideline #2:
Analyze, Analyze, Analyze

"Go with your gut" is terrible advice, which is not to say that your gut instinct will always be a bad one. A gut instinct can be based on years of experience and accumulated wisdom. But if you're going to take a risk that could be a disaster if it doesn't pan out, you need to have more than a "feeling" about it.

> If you're going to take a risk that could be a disaster if it doesn't pan out, you need to have more than a "feeling" about it.

When Moses led the Israelites to the border of the Promised Land, he had every reason to believe they would be able to cross the Jordan River into the land and take it from the tribes that were already living there because God had promised that he would help them. Still, he felt inclined to study the situation. He selected twelve men, the best and brightest, one from each of the twelve tribes, and sent them into the land on an intelligence-gathering mission. They were spies in the truest sense, long before anyone had ever heard of James Bond or Jack Ryan.

If you know your Old Testament history, you know that the Israelites chickened out and refused to cross into the land. Still, Moses demonstrated why he was God's choice to lead the Israelites. He wasn't a knee-jerk kind of leader. Even when he knew his gut feeling was strong, he still did his homework.

One of the most important reasons you need to thoroughly analyze your situation is so that if the risk you take doesn't work out, you will not be burdened with regrets. It's been said that the two most painful words in the English language are "if only."

"If only I'd looked at the situation more closely ... "

"If only I hadn't been in such a hurry ... "

"If only I'd asked a few more questions ... "

"If only I'd known what happened before ... "

The world is full of leaders who undermined their own success by letting a feeling of urgency drive a key decision instead of taking their time and analyzing all the available information.

Guideline #3:
Be Sensitive to Timing

Sometimes the problem is not with the idea itself but with the timing.

It was in the 1930s that radios started showing up in cars. You might think a young, forward-thinking entrepreneur in those days would have foreseen the popularity of the car radio, jumped right into the business, and made a fortune. But that's not the way it happened.

For years lawmakers, and especially insurance companies, fought the idea of installing radios in cars. Their belief was that drivers would become so engrossed in what they were listening to that they wouldn't be paying attention to their driving. Dire predictions of mass accidents, injuries, and death were promoted across the land. Obviously, that's not what happened. But it took several years for that battle to be fought in our culture and for the car radio to gain wide acceptance. The point is that if you had gotten into the car radio business in the 1930s, you probably would have gone broke. But if you had gotten into it in the 1940s, you probably would have gotten rich.

If you have a risky idea, ask yourself if the timing is right.

Is the idea ahead of its time? That's okay, as long as it's not so far ahead of its time that people won't be able to understand it. Maybe you need to wait until you have time to educate your people on the need.

Is your economic situation healthy enough to sustain the idea? History is full of examples of great ideas that fizzled because the money ran dry. Maybe you need to wait until your finances are on more solid footing.

> **There is such a thing as a great idea that isn't a great idea right now.**

Is your staff sufficient to handle the increased workload? Your people will not be happy if you pile more work on them. Even if you offer a raise in pay, they may resent the longer hours and the additional stress on their family lives. Maybe you need to wait until you can afford to add staff to implement the idea.

There is such a thing as a great idea that isn't a great idea right now.

Guideline #4:
Don't Assume That What Worked for Someone Else Will Work for You

This is one of the easiest leadership mistakes to make. You read an article about an innovative company that launched a revolutionary program that produced incredible results. Or you go to a conference and hear a testimonial about some new technique that launched a company like yours to the next level. And immediately you think, "We could do that!" But the question is "*Should* you do that?"

The answer is "Not necessarily."

It's the old apples and oranges comparison. The demographic of the community you operate in might be drastically different from the company you want to emulate. The people you employ might be of a completely different mindset. The strengths and weakness of your organization might be completely different. The competition you face might be much greater than what the other company faced. Any one of these factors could doom your effort.

Most likely what you'll need to do is adapt the idea to your situation. Make it fit your demographic and personnel and culture.

Guideline #5:

Make Sure the Risk You're Contemplating Offers a Sufficient Reward

I think about this every time I see a picture of somebody doing something extremely dangerous simply for the chance to get a cool selfie.

Vishnu and Meenakshi Moorthy were software engineers from India who also did some travel blogging. Their passion was photographing themselves perched on the edges of steep cliffs and skyscrapers. They would get as close as possible without falling to their deaths and then snap the picture. In October 2019 they were killed when they fell eight hundred feet from a cliff in Yosemite National Park.[7]

Sadly, there is a growing subculture in our social media–driven world that believes the quickest way to go viral is simply to post a picture of some death-defying stunt. Some are killed and many are injured, all for the chance to impress people on social media whom they don't even know.

There is a point at which every risk-taker should ask him- or herself, "Is it worth it? If I am successful, will it be worth what I stand to lose if I fail?" This can be a very hard question. For example, if what

---

7 Mike Elgan, "People Are Falling Off Buildings in Search of the Perfect Instagram Shot," *Fast Company*, January 4, 2019, https://www.fastcompany.com/90287323/people-are-falling-off-buildings-in-search-of-the-perfect-instagram-shot.

you stand to lose is your life, many would say no risk is worth it. But is that always true?

When young David decided to take on Goliath, everyone around him tried to talk him out of it. They thought he would be crushed like a bug under the heel of the mighty giant. But David felt that standing up for what was right in that moment was worth whatever risk he might have to take.

I would never say you shouldn't risk your life. Millions of people have risked their lives in noble causes, including the fight for and defense of freedom. But you need to make sure that the goal you have in mind for yourself or your company is worth what it could cost you. If it is, fine. Go for it. But if it isn't, please use some common sense and step away from the ledge.

Guideline #6:
Don't Be a Slave to Conventional Wisdom

This is a ticklish one to talk about because wisdom is critical in anything you do. We all need all the wisdom we can get! But *conventional* wisdom, by definition, is a thought or idea that has grown out of what has become generally accepted.

Remember, it was once generally accepted that the earth was flat.

It was once generally accepted that draining blood out of sick people made them well.

It was once generally accepted that people with dark skin were inferior.

It was once generally accepted that man would never be able to fly.

You get the idea.

It's best to be wary of conventional wisdom. It could be a trap.

Just ask Bill Gates.

He was attending Harvard. *Harvard.* How many people would love to go to Harvard but will never get the opportunity? Conventional wisdom would say that if you get into Harvard, you are blessed beyond words. Only a fool would get in and then drop out. But that's exactly what Bill Gates did in 1975. But he didn't drop out to sit on his parents' couch and watch TV. He dropped out to start a little company called Microsoft. He had a dream to make computers personal, to put one in every home, to make computing accessible to people in all walks of life. Who knows how our lives might be different if he had been a slave to conventional wisdom?

What was perfect wisdom for one person may not be for you.

Please note that I said above that it's best to be *wary* of conventional wisdom. I didn't say you should ignore it or reject it out of hand. It must have *some* wisdom in it or it wouldn't have become conventional in the first place. But times change, technologies change, people's attitudes and needs change. What was perfect wisdom at one time may not be so anymore. What was perfect wisdom for one person may not be for you.

Guideline #7:
Once You've Decided to Take a Risk, Go For It with Everything You've Got

Somebody once observed that the world's highways are littered with flat squirrels that were only halfway committed. There's just something about being hesitant and tentative that brings failure, and not just for squirrels. In almost every area of life, success goes to those people who know what they want and go after it full bore. The world tends to get out of the way and accommodate people who are boldly moving forward. The one thing you don't want to do is have your effort fall flat and then have to wrestle with the regret that comes from knowing you could have tried harder or put more into it. If your risk is going to fail, let it be for some reason other than a lack of passion and effort.

And understand that the energy to create this passion and effort has to radiate from you, the leader. George W. Bush was speaking for leaders everywhere in all kinds of situations when he said this in the aftermath of 9/11: "A president has to be the calcium in the backbone. If I weaken, the whole team weakens. If I'm doubtful, there will be doubt. If my confidence level in our ability declines, it will send ripples throughout the whole organization."[8] How true! You as the leader need to exemplify the kind of passion and energy you want to see in your team.

I want to wrap up this chapter with a word of encouragement to those leaders who may not be young anymore. Comedy writers Martha Bolton and Brad Dickson wrote a book called *Race You to the Fountain of Youth* (Howard Publishing, 2007). In that book they describe some of the sure signs of aging. One is watching reruns of *The Brady Bunch* and suddenly realizing that you identify with Sam the Butcher more than Peter Brady. Another is that you have a date with a woman who says you remind her of her father … only your hair is grayer. Aging does change things, I can surely attest to that. Just don't let it rob you of your spirit of adventure and your willingness to take a risk.

When I retired from the Orlando Magic in 2019, people who didn't know me probably thought I would be spending most of my time in my slippers, kicked back in a recliner, using the TV remote to jump from game to game. In fact, I began working on two projects that are very important to me: The Pat Williams Leadership Library and bringing Major League Baseball to Orlando. Both projects bear some risk in that they will require tons of work and yet still hinge on

---

8 Bob Woodward, *Bush at War* (New York: Simon & Schuster, 2002).

key factors falling into place, some of which are beyond our control. But to me, it's worth it. I find it exciting to think that a couple of my greatest life accomplishments could happen after my eightieth birthday.

Obviously, there are some risks you should not take as an older person, like getting up on a ladder to clean out your gutters. But it would be a shame if you allowed a lifetime of knowledge and experience to go to waste in your golden years. You have a deep reservoir of wisdom that has tremendous value. Don't be reluctant to use it. Keep pushing the envelope.

Besides, why should those young whippersnappers have all the fun?

CHAPTER 4

Reluctant to Mentor

The word "mentor" comes from Homer's *Odyssey*. It's the story of Odysseus's ten-year adventure following the Trojan War. While he was away from home, Odysseus entrusted the care of his son to a friend, asking him to guide, educate, and care for the boy. His trusted friend's name was Mentor, which is why today we refer to anyone who teaches and guides someone in a one-on-one relationship as a mentor.

When I look into a mirror, I see the face of a man whose life might have turned out much differently if not for the influence of a few key mentors. Allow me to introduce them to you.

One was "Mom" Burgher. I met her in 1962 when I was a student at Indiana University in Bloomington. She and her husband, Bob, owned Burgher's Grill on Main Street. If you're thinking "fifties diner," you're spot on. It could have been the set of *Happy Days*. I never saw Richie and Potsie and Ralph Malph there, but they would have fit right in.

The funny thing about Mom Burgher was that she had no biological kids of her own but became a mother figure to countless students simply by being kind and open and willing to talk about anything without being judgmental. We all knew we were welcome to stop by her house at any time of the day or night if we needed to talk. She would offer a bite to eat and a listening ear, then offer some piece of advice that always made perfect sense. I remember always walking away from those chats feeling ready to take on the world. Given how challenging a person's college years can be, Mom Burgher was just the person I needed at that time in my life.

The next key influencer in my life was Bill Durney. I met him when I was playing minor league baseball in Miami. He was the general manager of the team then called the Miami Marlins, a class A affiliate of the Phillies. As previously stated, my baseball abilities were not the stuff of legend. But the organization did see some leadership potential in me, so after a couple of less-than-stellar seasons behind the plate, I was transitioned to the team's front office.

I still remember the day I asked Bill to help me understand the business side of professional baseball. He was a busy man and could have told me to get lost. Instead, he took me under his wing and poured his knowledge into me. I was a sponge. I can honestly say that everything I know about sports management I learned from Bill Durney. But one of the most important things he did for me was introduce me to Bill Veeck.

William Louis Veeck Jr. is a sports legend, perhaps the most famous promoter, innovator, and franchise owner in baseball history. He was such an outside-the-box thinker that he became known for crazy tactics and wild publicity stunts. You might remember that he once signed Eddie Gaedel, who was less than four feet tall, to a professional contract and inserted him into a big-league game to draw a walk, which he did. Bill once said, "I try not to break the rules, merely to test their elasticity."

I met Bill Veeck when I was twenty-two. He became a friend, counselor, and adviser who imparted mountains of wisdom. Even years later, when I was well into my NBA career, I found myself seeking his advice and encouragement.

But perhaps the most important influencer I met along the way was Mr. R. E. Littlejohn. He was the owner of the Spartanburg Phillies when I was the team's general manager. I remember when I first got to town, I stopped by his house to introduce myself. His wife met me at the door and informed me that he was out of town. She also told me that I would never meet another man like him. She was right.

My father had recently passed away, and Mr. R. E. all but adopted me, treating me like the son he never had. As we worked together and became closer as friends, I had countless occasions to observe his spotless character in action. I also drank in his extraordinary wisdom, which was more profound than any I had encountered up to that point. His influence on me was so far-reaching that, years later, we actually named our firstborn son James Littlejohn Williams.

Given what I've just told you, it will come as no surprise that I am a big believer in mentoring. I've also studied history and know what a huge role mentoring has played in shaping people and accomplishments. Think about Jesus and his disciples. Talk about guys who did great things! But none of it would have happened without a three-year mentoring period that we read about in the gospels. Jesus molded and shaped his guys thoughtfully and carefully until they were ready to take over in his absence. And keep in mind, at first glance the guys he was mentoring were not cut out for what he wanted them to do. They weren't preachers and theologians who had just graduated from seminary; they were fishermen and tax collectors. But careful mentoring shaped them for the tasks they would face.

I must also mention the grand trio of Greek philosophers: Socrates, Plato, and Aristotle. How many times have you heard them quoted? They were towering intellects who lived a few hundred years before Christ. What you may not know is that they form a mentoring chain. Socrates mentored Plato, who in turn mentored Aristotle. And then Aristotle got into the mentoring act himself, tutoring Alexander the Great. Most Americans fail to realize how profoundly these men shaped Western thought. So much of how we view politics, logic, rhetoric, art, and beauty has its roots in the philosophical meanderings of these intellectual giants.

A more recent example of mentoring would be Oprah Winfrey's relationship with her fourth-grade teacher Mrs. Duncan. Oprah said, "One of the defining moments of my life came in the fourth grade, the year I was Mrs. Duncan's student. What Mrs. Duncan did for me was help me to not be afraid of being smart. She encouraged me to read, and she often stayed after school to work with me, helping me choose books and letting me help her grade papers."[9] Oprah turned out to be pretty smart indeed. She is perhaps the world's leading media executive, lending her talents to countless pursuits, including acting, producing, hosting a talk show, and serving mankind as a philanthropist.

I could go on, but I think you get the idea. Scroll through the pages of history and you will find mentoring relationships right and left among the world's most successful and influential people. Mentoring can lift and empower people like almost nothing else. And the mentor benefits too. Respect, the personal satisfaction that comes from helping others, and greater efficiency are just a few of the positive results

---

9 James C. Price, "Great Mentor Relationships throughout History," Refresh Leadership, January 13, 2015, http://www.refreshleadership.com/index.php/2015/01/great-mentor-relationships-history/.

mentors will see as they lift and encourage the people around them. Every leader ought to be a mentor!

But many are reluctant to take on the role. Allow me to share with you the three main comments reluctant mentors will make.

"I don't have the time." People who have valuable knowledge and experience to share are generally very busy. They are important people doing important things. This does not mean, however, that they don't have time to mentor someone. It might seem counterintuitive, but mentoring really isn't about how much time you have; it's about how much you love people.

The late Rich DeVos was the cofounder of the Amway organization and the principal owner of the Orlando Magic. A busy guy, to say the least. Yet he still found time to mentor countless people. His former son-in-law Bob Vander Weide said, "Why is Rich a mentor to so many people? Because he can't help himself! He loves people so much, and he wants to see them succeed." It's like anything else in life—you find time for the things you love. We all do. I, for example, love to read. Even on my busiest days at the peak of my career, I found time to plow through some pages. I know busy people who love to work out. Even when their schedules are packed, they find time to get to the gym. That old saw "I just don't have time" is seldom true. More often, it is just a phrase we trot out to keep from having to explain why we're not doing something we should be doing.

"It's basically just glorified babysitting, and I have more important things to do." When I hear this statement, I know the speaker has no understanding of mentoring. Mentoring is about as far as you can get from babysitting. Babysitting is holding the fort until the parents get home. Keep the kids from destroying things and killing each other and you can walk out the door knowing you've succeeded. Mentoring, on the other hand, is building. It's taking a person who has potential and

helping him or her reach it. When you walk away from a babysitting job, you feel good if nothing bad happened. When you walk away from a mentoring relationship, you feel incredible because something wonderful happened. That person you were working with blossomed. Potential was turned into power and purpose. And if it's your company the person works for, you just gained a much more effective employee!

"I will reduce my own value to the organization." This one kind of makes sense, doesn't it? If you work hard for years to gain knowledge and experience, then give it away to some young tiger the company just hired, won't you be hurting yourself? Imagine you are an aging baseball player trying to squeeze a few more years out of your career. In spring training you meet the young hotshot, the kid with loads of talent but no polish. The curveball still gives him trouble, and his footwork around the first base bag needs to be refined. If you were to take him under your wing and work with him, wouldn't you just be helping him take your job?

Maybe, and if your paycheck is all you care about, you'll hold the kid at arm's length. But if you can see beyond yourself, you'll understand that there's a blessing in giving yourself away that can't be measured in dollars or status.

Arturo Sandoval is arguably the world's greatest trumpet player, having won ten Grammy Awards and been nominated nineteen times. As a young Cuban musician, he met jazz legend Dizzy Gillespie, who took him under his wing and mentored him. Sandoval eventually defected to the United States and built a career that has touched virtually every musical medium, from live performances to recordings to film scores. What's beautiful is that Arturo can't open his mouth to speak about his career without heaping praise on Dizzy Gillespie.

What is the value of that?

When you come to the end of your life, those extra paychecks you may have gotten because you refused to mentor someone who seemed like a potential threat will pale in comparison to the praise that same person gives you because you were kind and concerned enough to help him along the way. Selflessness will enrich your life. Selfishness will shrivel you and make you lonely in your old age.

> Selflessness will enrich your life. Selfishness will shrivel you and make you lonely in your old age.

If you have felt reluctant to be a mentor, I suspect there are a couple of questions that have been swimming around in your head. Let me see if I can answer them.

Question #1:

Do I Even Have the Ability to Mentor Someone?

Mentoring is like anything else. Some people are good at it, and some people aren't. Let me run down a list of the five qualities the best mentors possess.

Quality #1: Positive Experience

A woman who'd been married and divorced several times was reflecting on her life in a conversation with a few friends. She lamented her marital failures but then added, "I feel like I've learned so much through my experiences. I'm thinking about writing a book that would help young women just starting out." None of her friends said anything, but to a person, they all thought, "Who would want marital advice from someone who's only ever had horrible marriages?" I'm not suggesting that in order to be a good mentor you have to be the best at what you do, but you certainly shouldn't be the worst!

If you've been to New York City, you know that the health department conducts surprise inspections of restaurants once a year. They measure compliance to rules about handling food, cleanliness, food temperatures, and employee hygiene. Each violation gets points; so the lower the score, the better the restaurant measures up. At the end of the inspection, the establishment is given a letter grade—A, B, or C—which they must post in the window. If you're ever walking the streets of Manhattan looking for something to eat, you will find yourself looking at those grades and steering clear of those C-rated establishments. Likewise, a leader who has a "C-rated" record will not find people lining up to be mentored. And that's as it should be. People are looking for someone with *positive* experience to share.

Quality #2: Good Character

This is different from positive experience. Matt Lauer, the former anchorman at NBC, had lots of positive experience. He reached the top of his profession, filling just about every role that is available to a TV "talking head." But it turned out that his character was horrible. His treatment of women in the workplace was far beyond inappropriate. I don't know any young journalist who would want to be mentored by Matt Lauer, even if he does know just about everything there is to know about the TV news business.

It is good to stay away from people with bad character, even if they are extremely talented. Monique Hennagan, Jearl Miles-Clark, and Tasha Colander-Richardson learned this lesson the hard way. They were members of the 1,600-meter relay team that won a gold medal in the 2000 Olympics. They lived with the joy of that accomplishment until 2008, when they were stripped of their medals because it was confirmed that the fourth member of their team, Marion Jones, used performance enhancing drugs.

I'll put it as simply as I can. It doesn't matter how gifted you are. It doesn't matter how many trophies sit on your shelf. It doesn't matter how many accolades the world throws your way. If you cannot offer a daily example of good character to the person you are mentoring, don't mentor.

Quality #3: Authenticity

Remember the Wizard of Oz? Or as he called himself, the Great and Powerful Oz? The image he projected to the world was of a giant talking head with a swollen brain cavity surrounded by billowing smoke and lightning flashes. Scary stuff. Impressive but intimidating. Not the kind of person you want to get close to. It wasn't until Dorothy and her friends discovered the real man behind the curtain that they were able to connect in a meaningful way. Likewise, you must be willing to let the person you're mentoring see the real you, not just some manufactured version of you that is only for public consumption.

There's a story about a man who went to a marriage counselor. He said, "Doc, my wife is so hard to live with. I just don't know what to do." The doctor said, "I've met your wife, and she seems so nice. If I were going to pick a song that describes her, it would be 'Sweet Hour of Prayer.'" The man said, "Well, I live with her, and I can assure you that she's more 'Battle Hymn of the Republic' than 'Sweet Hour of Prayer.'"

If the person you're mentoring is only going to see the airbrushed and spit-polished version of you that you manufacture for public consumption, then there's really no point in having the relationship. Meaningful sharing happens when you decide to drop your mask and be real.

Quality #4: A Willingness to Invest

I mentioned earlier that Mr. R. E. Littlejohn was the owner of the Spartanburg Phillies when I was the team's young general manager. He was always willing to invest in me. He gave me his time and attention. Sometimes he even willingly suffered financially.

> If you're going to be a good mentor, you must be willing to give time and energy, but you must also be willing to let your mentee learn from doing, even if he or she doesn't always do it right.

I'm referring to my second year as the team's GM. I decided to go all-out with my promotions. I paid thousands of dollars to get celebrities like Bart Starr, Paul Hornung, Johnny Unitas, Bob Feller, Satchel Paige, and others to come and sign autographs. I spent Mr. R. E.'s money like there was no tomorrow, always expecting him to call me any minute and tell me to put on the brakes. But he never did, and I would eventually figure out why.

When the end of the season came, we'd had a great year with attendance way up. And we would have made a nice profit ... if my promotions hadn't gone way over budget. It suddenly, painfully dawned on me that my end-of-the-year bonus, which would have been very nice if I'd shown some restraint, was going to be miniscule because of my overspending. Mr. R. E. allowed me to spend, spend, spend because he knew at the end of the season I was going to learn a valuable lesson. At any point during the season he could have called me in and lectured me about the bottom line, but he was more interested in seeing me learn a powerful lesson than hanging onto a few more of his dollars.

If you're going to be a good mentor, you must be willing to give time and energy, but you must also be willing to let your mentee learn from doing, even if he or she doesn't always do it right.

Quality #5: Patience

You could list patience as an essential quality for just about any important endeavor, but it's especially important when trying to mentor someone. Mentoring is people work, and people will test your patience for sure. For one thing, they don't always learn as quickly as we'd like for them to, even if the raw talent is there. It's why the term "late bloomer" was coined. Or they might show the opposite tendency, which would be to bite off too much too soon, in which case they need to be reeled back in. Either way, the mentor will need patience. When working with people, things seldom go perfectly.

Positive experience, good character, authenticity, a willingness to invest, and patience. If you possess these qualities, congratulations! You're mentor material! But there's still another question that may be holding you back.

Question #2:
What Are the Dangers I Need to Avoid?

I can think of four.

Danger #1: Mentoring a Member of the Opposite Sex

We live in a very strange time. Our culture is sexually charged like never before while at the same time being sensitive to any word or act that could be construed to have even the slightest sexual connotation. Think about it. People sit at home and watch shows like *Game of Thrones* that feature brutally explicit scenes of rape and sexuality, then go to work and feel offended by a mildly off-color comment made around the watercooler. I'll leave it to the sociologists and theologians to explain this, but I will suggest that we are living in a time when it's very easy for interactions between the sexes to go sideways. Since the #MeToo movement was started, sexual harassment claims are up sharply. Many men confess to being confused, as words and actions that were once okay are no longer. I'm not saying it's impossible for a man and a woman to have a professional mentoring relationship, but I wonder if it's probably safer not even to try.

It sounds prudish, I know. But I've been around a long time, and I know the nature of attraction and the weakness of people. I know that a mentoring relationship can create scenarios where two people are alone and talking about deeply personal issues. I know emotion can get involved and that romantic sparks can fly when you least expect them. I know that people don't always use the best judgment in moments where strong feelings are surging. And most importantly, I know that sometimes one person feels a sexual or emotional attraction and the other person doesn't, creating the potential for an awkward or even relationship-ruining moment.

Again, I'm talking about mentoring *dangers* here. The risk of something uncomfortable or inappropriate happening increases significantly when sexual attraction is thrown into the mentoring mix. It just seems like a good idea to take that risk off the table. And this is especially true if you are married. Don't make your spouse sit at home and wonder if there's an undercurrent of sexual attraction in your mentoring relationship. Even if there isn't, your spouse will still wonder, and nothing good can come from that. Every time his or her mind creates a possible romantic scenario between you and your mentee—and in all likelihood that *will* happen—the quality of your marriage will tick down a notch. It just isn't worth it.

Danger #2: Mentoring Someone with Profound Character Flaws

As a leader you want to invest your mentoring time and energy in someone who is worthy of what you have to offer. You want to impart your knowledge and experience to someone who is ready to start doing something with it. That will not be the case if the person you're mentoring has character flaws that sit in opposition to your personal values and the core values of your organization.

Sometimes people make a great first impression. Who among us hasn't been fooled by that person who has a great personality and seems to know all the right things to say? It can happen so easily, which is why many churches and organizations have rules that prevent someone from being moved into a position of leadership until a one-year probationary period has passed. But even then, sometimes a person with a dark side can slip through the cracks. Judas is an example. Jesus mentored him along with his other eleven disciples, but all that teaching and encouragement was wasted as Judas turned on Jesus and collaborated with his enemies.

People with serious character flaws may need counseling or rehabilitation. Let them get it and prove that they have straightened themselves out before you start pouring into them. It is a privilege to be mentored, and people need to earn that privilege.

Danger #3: Mentoring Someone Who Isn't Teachable

Ron Hunter Jr. and Michael Waddell wrote a brilliant book called *Toy Box Leadership*. In it, they talk about ten iconic toys and what they have to teach us about leadership. In their chapter on mentoring, they focus on Play-Doh. According to their research, more than a billion pounds of Play-Doh have been manufactured since it was first invented. In case you're wondering, that would be enough Play-Doh to roll out a "snake" that would reach around the world three times![10]

Play-Doh was a perfect choice for their chapter on mentoring because it is moldable. When you set out to mentor someone, that's exactly what you're looking for, someone who not only can be shaped but is also willing to be shaped. Unfortunately, a lot of people aren't. They will tell you they are, but as time goes by you'll see evidence of resistance. You'll notice that nothing is changing or that they constantly want to argue for their own point of view. And don't forget body language. Unteachable people will usually be good for a sigh and an eye roll at some point during every conversation.

If you find yourself trying to mentor someone like this, you might as well pull the plug and move on because you are wasting your time. And don't fool yourself into believing that the person will eventually come around and begin to embrace what you're trying to impart. People are either teachable or they're not. Yes, they can change, but they need to change *before* they start taking up your time. The only thing you will get out of trying to mentor an unteachable person is frustration, and if you're a leader, you probably have enough of that already. Save yourself the time and trouble.

Danger #4: Trying to Clone Yourself

If you haven't given it some thought ahead of time, you can become frustrated as a mentor. You can start sharing with your mentee how you think and what you do, expecting him or her to start adopting your approach and your style. Then, when that doesn't happen, you start thinking, "Why am I wasting my time? I'm obviously not

---

10 Run Hunter Jr. and Michael Waddell, *Toy Box Leadership* (Nashville: Thomas Nelson, 2008), 40.

getting through." But the point of mentoring is not to create a clone of yourself. The point of mentoring is to help someone reach his or her unique potential. Much of what you impart to your mentee will be processed, not duplicated. It will be blended in with his or her own thoughts and skills and personality.

Think about musicians. When one mentors another, there is no expectation that the mentee will sound exactly like the mentor. The mentee will not copy the mentor's sound and style. What would be the fun in that? Rather, the mentee will process what he learns and blend it in with everything else he knows and believes about music. This is why a jazz aficionado can hear a sax player who doesn't sound like John Coltrane but know that he has listened to a lot of Coltrane. He's not mimicking the tenor sax legend, but the influence is there.

I can assure you that I am not a clone of the four mentors I mentioned at the top of this chapter. But if you know me and had known them, you would definitely be able to tell that they influenced me.

Times have changed so much since I first became a leader. In the old days, we interacted with people face to face. We actually looked each other in the eye and spoke words. They're called conversations. You may have heard of them. Now most people think the best way to interact with others is through social media. They mistakenly think that the number of social media followers they have is a reflection of their importance, of their influence. The problem with social media is that while you may be able to reach thousands of people with a single tweet, the impact is so miniscule that it hardly makes a difference. Why? Because that person who just received your tweet likely received dozens of others at the same time! You'll be lucky if he or she gives your tweet two or three seconds of consideration.

Mentoring, by contrast, goes much deeper. You spend time together. You talk. You collaborate. You grow. And when the time comes to move on to the next stage of your life, you do so as a changed person. And most likely with a friend that you will have forever. There is really no downside to the kind of mentoring I've described in this chapter, either for the mentor or the mentee. All it takes is the willingness to do it.

CHAPTER 5

Reluctant to Confront

Confrontation has a long history.

A *real* long history.

All the way back in the Garden of Eden, God approached Adam and said, "Have you eaten from the tree whose fruit I commanded you not to eat?"

He admitted that he had, God responded with some curses as punishment, and nothing was ever the same for the human race.

Then, in the very next chapter, God confronted Adam's son Cain, not once but twice. When Cain was moping around looking dejected, God said, "Why are you so angry?" And then later, after Cain had lured his brother Abel into the wilderness and bludgeoned him to death, God said to Cain, "Where is your brother?"

That makes three major confrontations in the first three-plus chapters of the Bible, which I see as a pretty strong endorsement from God regarding the effectiveness of confrontation as a tool for addressing and correcting bad attitudes and behavior. And we know it is. Every leadership expert I've ever heard of hammers away at the importance of confrontation because when it *doesn't* happen, five terrible things always result.

First, problem people are empowered. Ever see a two-year-old completely controlling his parents in a supermarket or department store? It's a thing to behold, isn't it? That little bitty kid who can't even change his own pants has full-grown adults doing whatever he wants. Where does the little squirt get that kind of power? From his parents! They grant it to him by failing to confront his screaming temper tantrums.

You can take it to the bank: problem people are always empowered when no one confronts them. From the two-year-old in the grocery store to the terrorist organization in the Middle East, fail to stand up to them and their bad behavior will get worse every time.

Second, when confrontation doesn't happen, morale sinks like the Titanic. Low morale in any organization is generally caused by two emotions mixing together: irritation and frustration. Irritation because someone (or perhaps a group of people) is causing problems, and frustration because the people who could do something about it are letting it slide. And nothing reduces the effectiveness of a team like low morale. When people are irritated and frustrated, they lose heart. When they lose heart, they stop caring. And when they stop caring, the business or organization becomes like a dead man walking. The doors may remain unlocked and the lights on, but there is no life inside.

Third, when confrontation doesn't happen, leaders lose respect. Imagine renting a house. At some point after you move in, the roof starts leaking and the water heater goes on the blink. You call the landlord, assuming he will have repairs made promptly, but he doesn't. So, day after day you shower in cold water, and when it rains, you set out pots and pans to catch the drips. How much respect are you going to have for your landlord?

The same thing happens with businesses and organizations. If the leader doesn't address the problems—and especially the problem people—who are making the workplace an unpleasant environment, he or she will lose the respect of everyone who works there.

Fourth, when confrontation doesn't happen, the leader will gain a bad reputation, which will make it hard for him to keep and attract good people. You can see this in the sports world. Teams that have a dysfunctional culture that never seems to get fixed have a hard time hanging on to good players and attracting quality free agents. Even if the money is good, players that are good enough to have multiple offers don't want to be a part of a soap opera. They'll often take less money to be part of a healthy environment. It happens in nonsports organizations too. Right now millions of people are looking for new jobs because they want to escape a miserable culture at their current place of employment.

Fifth, when confrontation doesn't happen, success is subverted. I don't know of a single organization of any kind that can thrive with unhappy employees in a dysfunctional environment. In fact, many businesses fail not because they don't offer a needed product or service but because the internal sickness of the company poisons the whole operation and kills it. I would say that 95 percent of the time that sickness got its start when a leader somewhere back in the organization's past failed to confront a problem … or the person behind the problem.

I'm not going to say that no leader likes confrontation, because there is that rare person who seems to relish it. You know the type: nothing makes him happier than a chance to flex his leadership muscles and show people who's boss. But it's safe to say that the vast majority of leaders hate confrontation and will avoid it if they possibly can.

Eight Reasons Why Leaders Avoid Confrontation

It's not just because confrontation is hard that leaders avoid it. I've identified eight other reasons why leaders are reluctant to do it.

Reason #1: Naïve Optimism

The leader thinks that if he or she just sits tight, the problem will take care of itself. After all, people are basically good, right? Just leave them alone and they'll find their way through whatever the problem is and everything will be okay.

Ha. Ha. Ha.

Murphy's Law says that whatever can go wrong will go wrong. Here's Pat's Law: Whatever is going wrong will continue to go wrong until it's fixed. In fact, if the situation is not addressed, it will only get worse. Any belief to the contrary is foolishness, pure and simple.

Whatever is going wrong will continue to go wrong until it's fixed.

Understand that everything—*everything*—deteriorates. I can remember when I squatted down behind home plate and dug balls out of the dirt. Now if I tried to squat down behind home plate, someone would have to dig *me* out of the dirt! I'm deteriorating, and so are you! Yes, everything deteriorates. Did you mow your grass recently? I hate to tell you this, but you're going to have to mow it again real soon. Did you change the oil in your car? Better make an appointment at the service center because it's going to need to be done again or your engine will start to break down. Everything deteriorates, and that includes problems. Only in some fantasy world do they just magically get better on their own. If your strategy for dealing with problems is to sit tight and hope for the best, you are headed for some dark days.

Reason #2: Fear of the Person Who Needs Confronting

Let's face it—some people are just intimidating. If you know a person is a hothead or just doesn't take criticism well, it can make you not want to confront him. Maybe you've witnessed previous explosions or heard stories about the person's heated overreactions. Hotheaded people usually develop quite a reputation, causing people to walk on eggshells around them. Sometimes they develop an aura of invincibility because no one has the courage to confront them about anything.

Keep in mind that many people purposely cultivate this type of reputation, not just because it feeds their ego to know that they intimidate people but also because they understand how it serves them. It keeps their critics at bay. It causes their peers to defer to them and cater to their wishes so as not to make them mad. If you've ever been on a playground where there was a bully, you know how this works. It can present a real challenge for any leader.

Reason #3: The Productivity of the Person Who Needs Confronting

You might say, "But if a person is difficult to deal with, why don't you just fire him?" Great idea! Unless that person is your top producer. What if he is setting sales records every month? What if he is your top recruiter? What if his ideas have made your company much more efficient and profitable? What if you make him mad and he decides to walk? And what if he takes his talent and his ideas and his clients and starts working for your competitor? All of a sudden, firing him isn't so easy.

If you've ever wondered how obnoxious people keep their jobs, this is it: by producing! Even in sports. There are players who give their coaches and managers headaches and disrupt team chemistry, but because they hit thirty-five homers a year or score twenty points a game or rush for a thousand yards every season, those who would otherwise confront them look the other way. It's amazing what leaders are willing to put up with to keep a top producer in the fold.

Reason #4: The "Following" of the Person Who Needs Confronting

This one comes into play quite often in church. You've got a staff member who is wildly popular with a segment of the congregation. A youth minister, for example. But while the kids love him, he doesn't work well with the rest of the staff, his integrity has been shown to be questionable at best, and he's blown off some specific directions given to him by his supervisor. It's time to confront him, right? But if you do, and if you make him mad, and if he decides to quit or play the martyr, you know all of his students and probably their parents are going to take his side. At best they will be angry, and at worst they could all pack up and leave the church.

Many leaders make a calculated gamble at this point. They decide that it will be better for the organization in the long run if they just put up with the problem person's dysfunctions and learn to live with them rather than stirring up a big hornet's nest that might set the organization back several years. There are many problems with this approach, not the least of which is that left unconfronted the problem person's failures will always get worse. (See Reason #1: Everything Deteriorates.) Doing nothing might be okay—*might* be okay—if you knew a person's weaknesses would stay as they were. Maybe you could just bite your tongue and learn to live with them. But they won't stay as they are. They will get worse. What starts as an irritation will eventually become a problem, which will eventually become a disaster.

Reason #5: An Experience Deficit on the Part of the Leader

I was hired to lead the front office of the Philadelphia 76ers, Chicago Bulls, and Atlanta Hawks, three established professional sports organizations. At each of those stops, when I walked through the door on my first day, everyone in the office had seniority on me. Every single employee knew things I didn't know. Every one of them could look me in the eye and legitimately say, "I know more about what goes on here than you do." That would eventually change, of course. But for that moment, I needed them. And when you need someone, it can be hard to confront them. What if they get mad and quit? You can always hire someone else, of course. But you won't find someone with the same understanding of the system, which may be critical to your success at that moment.

There's also the awkward situation of having a legend on your team, someone who's been around forever, someone who's "done it all" with great success but is now slipping and not delivering the goods. Undying respect is owed to such a person, but how long can you ignore the elephant in the room? The last thing you want is to be perceived as being unkind or disrespectful to someone who means so much to the organization. This has prevented many a leader from having that hard conversation.

Reason #6: A Lack of Good Options

The following thought has gone through millions of leaders' minds: "If I confront him and he quits, then what do I do?" Some positions are easy to fill, obviously. But some aren't. Faith-based organizations learn this very quickly. Not only are they looking for people with outstanding skills (which can be hard enough to find); they also need people with the requisite spiritual credentials. Suddenly, their prospect list is trimmed by two-thirds!

You've seen the many advertisements about companies that will help you find just the right candidate for your open position. They make it sound so easy. List your job and in no time qualified candidates will be lining up at your door. But what if you're a small church or company and the "perfect" candidate lives two thousand miles away and you can't afford to relocate him to your area and offer him the pay package he's accustomed to? Sometimes leaders look at their options and simply sigh and say, "I better just keep quiet and live with what I've got." It's like when your mother makes you eat your spinach. You don't want it, but you don't have a lot of options, so you might as well learn to like it.

Reason #7: The Fear of Being Counterconfronted

There are three words that strike fear in the heart of many leaders who need to confront someone on their team. They are "What about you?" This happens when they know, even as they prepare to confront someone whose job performance isn't up to par, that they are on shaky ground themselves. For example, how do you confront an employee about being habitually late when you're rarely on time yourself? How do you confront an employee about his or her treatment of coworkers when many of the people who work for you think of you as being overly demanding or unsympathetic to their needs? As a leader you must understand that it's great to hold people accountable but the first person you need to hold accountable is yourself.

If you're a parent, you understand this very well. If you curse, you're not going to take a hard line against your child when he or she blurts out a bad word because you know what will happen. Your child will say, "But *you* say it!" And you know that any explanation you offer at that point will be totally lame. Even young children are perceptive enough to see such a glaring double standard. To avoid such embarrassing moments in the workplace, some leaders just find it easier to let things slide.

Lee Ellis is a retired United States Air Force colonel who was a prisoner of war in Vietnam and is now an award-winning author and speaker. He said, "Leadership, at every level, must be able to withstand scrutiny. Good leaders should welcome this type of accountability because it helps them succeed over the long haul. Bad ones will try to avoid it because they know it will expose their true colors."

Reason #8: The Person Needing to Be Confronted Is a Friend or Relative

However hard it is to confront someone under normal circumstances, you can double it when the person you're confronting is a friend or relative. Often friends and relatives expect special treatment. They think their connection to the boss should earn them some special privilcgcs. Thc boss may not agrcc but at thc samc timc hc is fcarful of causing a rift in the relationship. This is why some companies don't allow family members to work together. One of the oldest clichés in business lore is the boss's son-in-law who is resented by practically everyone in the company because he's not held to the same standard as everyone else.

So, I've given you eight reasons why leaders are reluctant to confront. It should be noted that sometimes several of these reasons can work together. When that happens, the leader will experience an almost overpowering temptation to look the other way and ignore whatever attitude or behavior needs to be corrected. The challenge you face is to address the items on this list that pertain to you, fix the ones you have control over, and figure out a way to manage the rest.

What you must not do is ignore the problem or the problem person. As I've already stated, to do nothing is to guarantee that even bigger problems will come.

Seven Tips for Confronting People Properly

So, let's move beyond the problem and talk about the solution. Once you've worked through the issues listed above, technique becomes the central issue. You have someone that needs confronting, and you're ready to do it. What do you do?

Tip #1: Set Up a Face-to-Face Meeting

Whatever you do, don't try to handle the situation over the phone or through social media, which would be even worse. Don't send an email or a text message. Be man or woman enough to look the person in the eye and say what you need to say.

The major benefit of a face-to-face meeting is that you can deal with whatever response is forthcoming in real time. If you send an email, you have no idea what the person's reaction is to what you've said. Is he contrite? Angry? Confused? Does he have some follow-up questions or concerns? Are there some important factors he's aware of that you aren't? Is he calling his coworkers and blaspheming your name? You need to know what the response is, especially if it's bad. But you won't unless you're sitting in front of the person, looking him in the eye.

Also, a face-to-face meeting is a show of respect on your part. It says, "I care about you enough to sit down with you and try to find a path forward." You might be surprised at how much that fact alone will soften the person's response. A text or an email, on the other hand, is very cold. It feels like a drive-by, a hit-and-run attack, whether you mean for it to or not.

Tip #2: Pick an Appropriate Time and Place

Have you ever noticed how many television dramas have no sense of the appropriateness of time and place? For example, the scene is the White House. The president and the secretary of state are discussing a top-secret military operation. But they're not discussing it in the Oval Office or the Situation Room, as you would expect. Oh no, they're walking down the hallway with all kinds of staffers and secretaries walking by. And they're making no attempt to keep their voices down!

If it's true that there's an appropriate time and place for everything, then it's equally true that there's an *inappropriate* time and place for everything. I strongly urge you not to confront someone at a time or place that would prove embarrassing to your employee. Do not under any circumstances allow other employees to see or hear the conversation. And do not choose a time when the conversation has to be rushed. Conversations of this nature need to run their full course. Both you and the person you're talking to need to get everything out in the open. It is simply unfair to call someone on the carpet, lay out your criticism, and then say, "Oh, sorry, we're out of time."

I do, however, want to add one caveat. While it is often okay to confront people one-on-one, there may be times when having a witness in the room is advisable. This is especially true when the matters being discussed are particularly sensitive, inflammatory, or have legal ramifications. Also, if the person you're confronting is known to have anger or honesty issues and might come back later with false accusations about what was said or done in the meeting, it would be best to have someone else in the room. It is better to be safe than sorry.

Tip #3: Be Calm but Firm

Under no circumstances should you confront someone when your anger is boiling. If you do, you will almost certainly say something you'll regret. You must also go into the meeting with a firm determination not to allow yourself to be provoked. If the person you're confronting is of a certain type, he or she might intentionally try to draw some sort of inappropriate reaction from you that could be used against you later. You must be prepared for this and keep a cool head at all costs. Proverbs 15:1 says, "A gentle answer deflects anger."

At the same time, you must be firm. A common tendency for many leaders is to wilt in the moment. They think of all the strong points they're going to make ahead of time, but when the meeting actually happens, they turn to mush, perhaps because the employee walks in looking scared to death or suddenly bursts into tears. As a leader you must avoid leaving important things unsaid. You don't want to reflect on the meeting afterward and be kicking yourself because you didn't make the points you had on your list. Be calm. Be kind. But don't wimp out. If you do, you'll probably be back in that same situation real soon.

Tip #4: Equip Yourself with Specific Concerns and Examples

For example, don't say, "Your attitude needs improving." Instead say, "I've heard you complaining a lot lately. The other day at the watercooler, you were going on about the new schedule I set up." See the difference? The first statement is virtually meaningless because, at times, don't all of our attitudes need improving? The second statement is much more useful because it puts a specific action on the table for discussion. You can talk about what was said and why saying it in that place at that time was counterproductive to the team's goals.

I recommend that you go to your meeting with several examples that back up your point. Whether you use them all is something you will determine on the fly. You don't want to unnecessarily grind the person into the dust, but at the same time you want to make sure he understands the gravity of the situation. Use as many examples as you need to in order to get the message across.

Tip #5: Be Ready and Willing to Listen

Yes, it's true. If you're the boss, it's a dictatorship. You call the shots, and ultimately, your opinion is the only one that matters. But if you allow your employee to walk away from the meeting feeling that reality, you have done a poor job. The best way to keep your employee from feeling oppressed is to listen to what he or she has to say. When employees become disgruntled, it's often because they feel like they have no voice.

> **Never discount the possibility that your employee—even a difficult employee—has something to say that you need to hear.**

And here's something else. Never discount the possibility that your employee—even a difficult employee—has something to say that you need to hear. I've been around long enough to know that if you asked employees in all kinds of companies all across the country if there was something they wished their bosses better understood or would change about company policies and procedures, most of them would say yes. Your job is to hear—*really* hear—what's being said and evaluate the validity of it. It might be hogwash. But it might not.

In the end, however, you must leave no doubt about who the boss is. Listening is good. Learning is good. Changing things might even be good. But it won't be good if your employee walks out the door thinking he has manipulated you.

Tip #6: Go into the Meeting with a Plan

Telling your employee to shape up is not a plan. A plan looks like this:

- A clear statement of the problem: "The behavior in question is unacceptable and must be corrected."
- Action steps: "Here are some specific expectations I have going forward."
- Time to do what needs to be done: "Over the next few weeks, I will be monitoring the situation to make sure things change."
- A warning: "If things don't change, it will indicate to me that you're not a good fit for our team, and I will proceed accordingly."

There are at least three reasons why a specific plan is important. One is because you want to show your employee that there is a way out of the wilderness. If the person really does want to be successful in your organization, you will be giving him every opportunity. A second benefit is that you have something to refer back to if nothing changes and you need to let the person go. He will never be able to say you didn't tell him what was expected. And the third reason a plan is important is to ensure fairness. As a leader you are human and will naturally like some people better than others. A specific plan with action steps and a timetable will keep you from playing favorites. The person will either get with the program or not.

Tip #7: When the Meeting Is Over, Leave It There and Move On

Don't talk about it to other employees. Above all don't talk anymore about it with the person you had to confront. If you see him in the hallway, smile and offer a friendly greeting. The last thing you want to do is perpetuate the tension that such a meeting invariably creates. Do your best to show the individual that you're willing to let the situation be a part of the past if the necessary corrections are made.

Confrontation is like everything else: much easier if you have a plan and execute it. Too many leaders fly by the seat of their pants. That is, they handle problems and problem people on the fly, often allowing their emotions to play a larger role than they should. In such instances, things are often said that shouldn't be and other things that should be said aren't. The result is often a feeling of frustration for everyone involved. It doesn't have to be that way! Follow these tips and you won't go wrong.

Rich DeVos was the cofounder of Amway and the principal owner of the Orlando Magic. One day I had him on my radio show, and he told an interesting story about a period of time when he financially supported an older evangelist named Anthony Zeoli. Rich said that every Sunday morning his home phone would ring at 9:00 a.m. He would pick up the handset and say, "Good morning, Anthony" because it was always Anthony Zeoli calling to tell him how he'd spent his time that week and what he had accomplished. Rich often said to him, "Anthony, you don't need to call me every week and tell me what you're doing. I trust you." And Anthony would respond, "Oh yes I do because I want to be accountable. You support me, so that makes me accountable to you. Everybody should take accountability seriously."

Anthony had the right attitude. Everybody should be accountable.

But of course everybody isn't. Which means there will be times when you as a leader will have to hold them accountable. That means occasional confrontations. If you build a good culture in your business, church, or organization, they shouldn't need to happen too often. But when they do, there's a right way and a wrong way to do it. Do it the right way and your entire organization will benefit.

CHAPTER 6

Reluctant to Rock the Boat

There was a time when the Swiss made the best timepieces in the world. The gears and bearings and springs of their watches were manufactured with unmatched attention to detail. Plus, they were responsible for great innovations such as minute hands, second hands, and waterproofing. For the better part of the last century, no one could touch them when it came to making a great watch. Switzerland was the nine-hundred-pound gorilla in a room full of chimpanzees.

But its reign came to an end, and during the 1970s and 1980s, sales dropped and thousands of Swiss watchmakers hit the unemployment lines. Before long their competitor, Seiko, surpassed them in terms of production and profit. Why? Because a new development came along—quartz movement—and the Swiss turned up their noses at it. They decided that the status quo was good enough, and in so doing allowed more forward-thinking companies to pass them by.[11]

History is full of similar examples. Companies and organizations

11 James Emery White, *Rethinking the Church* (Grand Rapids: Baker, 1997), 20.

that are doing well get comfortable, are afraid to rock the boat, and suffer losses as a result.

Back in the 1990s, many churches fought what we now call the "music wars." Traditional organ and piano music had served the church well for many years, but suddenly a push was being made by younger people to bring guitars and drums into the Sunday morning worship service along with more contemporary songs. For some churches this was a boat-rocking experience that not even a rowboat in a hurricane could match. Many churches flat out refused to make the change for fear of alienating their longtime, faithful members. But history shows that those church leaders who did risk rocking the boat with a new approach to music quickly took the lead in attracting new worshipers. Now, thirty years later, most churches have made the transition and those "war years" seem like ancient history. But ask any pastor who went through them what they were like, and he will tell you some horror stories. It's been said that "hell hath no fury like a woman scorned." I know pastors who would say, "Hell hath no fury like an old church member whose hymns are taken away."

Boat-rocking is generally thought of in negative terms. Some see it as the equivalent of disturbing the peace. Boat-rockers are often labeled "instigators" or "troublemakers." But when it comes to leadership, boat-rocking is essential. Somebody said, "There are three kinds of people: those who make things happen, those who watch things happen, and those who wonder what happened." Boat-rockers make things happen. Show me a company or an organization that broke out of its doldrums and found great success, and I'll show you a company that got its boat rocked by someone who had a vision beyond the status quo.

This chapter is especially for the leader who has a hard time pulling the trigger on change. We are going to examine the fine art of boat-rocking and turn you into an expert.

Why Boats Need to Be Rocked

The place to start is with an understanding of why the status quo is not your friend. Comfort is something everybody likes, but it can be an organization's worst enemy. I can think of six reasons why the boat you're in right now needs to be rocked occasionally.

Reason #1: Prolonged Comfort Leads to Staleness

Staleness may not kill people, but it also doesn't excite them, and it certainly won't attract them. How many restaurant commercials have you seen that say, "Come in today and try our cold soup and stale bread!" On the contrary, every food advertisement you see shows food that is fresh and piping hot. People in the food business spend megabucks to have their recipes and dishes filmed and photographed by professionals to make them look as fresh and enticing as possible.

Successful leaders know that nobody likes things that are stale. This is why Target and McDonald's, two of our most iconic brands, have spent the last few years remodeling all of their stores. Think of the expense of that. But they knew they had to do it because their stores were looking worn and drab. Now, with most of the work complete, their places really pop. You can walk into a store you've been going to for years and it feels brand new. There is a freshness and an energy that just wasn't there before.

Reason #2: Prolonged Comfort Acts Like a Sedative

Ever walk into a business and find the employees moving around like sleepwalkers, acting bored and uninterested? They glance at you but don't smile or speak. When you ask them a question, they act almost annoyed by the intrusion. And when they check you out at the register, they barely mumble a thank-you.

Any time you encounter young, otherwise energetic people operating on "snooze control" in the workplace, you can be sure it's because the environment and business model have become stale. Anytime you have employees with glazed-over expressions going through the motions like they'd rather be anywhere other than where they are, you know the boat needs to be rocked.

Leaders would do well to remember that just because things are running smoothly and work is getting done, it doesn't mean the business or organization is healthy and vibrant. If your people are operating on autopilot, a vital component of success is missing. It's called positive energy. You can keep the doors open without it, but you can't thrive.

Reason #3: Prolonged Comfort Means You Are Falling behind the Competition

Ever wonder why two businesses offering identical products or services have different results? Why one fizzles and the other booms? There could be a number of factors, of course, but I will guarantee you that somewhere in the mix will be this very issue. To some degree, one of the businesses will be changing, evolving, creating exciting new pathways forward, while the other is kicking back enjoying its current level of success.

By the way, it's perfectly okay to "cap" your business at a certain level. If that's all you want or can handle, fine. But if the idea is to compete in the marketplace, some boat-rocking will have to be done. If your competitors are introducing new products and services while you sit back and do what you've always done, they will pass you by.

Reason #4: Prolonged Comfort Preserves Your Weak Points

Think about what you do when you take a selfie, or when someone else takes your picture. In this day of camera phones, you can check right then to make sure the picture is good, that your eyes are open and you don't have a goofy expression on your face. If the picture is not to your liking, you can delete it with a tap of the screen and try again. The main thing is that you don't want something unattractive captured and preserved for all time.

Boat-rocking is what keeps unattractive things from being captured and preserved in your business or organization. For example, there is a restaurant in Orlando that has excellent food, but its restroom needs remodeling. The flooring is old and tarnished, the fixtures are dull and stained, and the paint on the wall looks like it was new during the Carter administration. It doesn't matter how hard they scrub that bathroom; it's going to look dingy and off-putting. It is by far the most unpleasant aspect of the restaurant. And what have they done? By failing to remodel, they have perpetuated that unpleasantness. They have locked it in. They have made their weakest point a permanent part of their identity.

Right now I'm sure you can think of businesses or organizations or churches that have glaring weaknesses and have had them for years. It's like when you go into someone's home and detect a strange smell. You think, "Wow, they need to open the windows and air this place out." But they don't notice. They're used to it. They're comfortable with it. And so the odor lives on. And on. And on.

Reason #5: Prolonged Comfort Stifles Creativity

One of the signs of a healthy culture is that your team members come to you with ideas on how to make things better. For one thing, it shows that they are invested in what you're trying to do. For another, it opens the possibility of something explosive happening. Who knows when that one idea might come along that will change everything? But there won't be any such ideas coming along if your people believe that the care and maintenance of the status quo is all you're looking for.

People generally adjust to whatever expectations are placed on them. If you hand a man a shovel and tell him to move a dirt pile from point A to point B, he'll do it. If you tell him to figure out the best way to move the dirt pile, he'll approach the job with an entirely different mindset. Part of being a good leader is unleashing your people. They may well have more to offer than you realize.

Reason #6: Prolonged Comfort Ignores Trends

The word "trendy" is sometimes used in a derogatory sense, as if to say something won't be popular for very long because it's just a fad and therefore doesn't need to be taken seriously. There can be some truth in this, but leaders are still wise to pay attention to trends. If your industry is leaning in a certain direction and you aren't, you can quickly fall behind and become irrelevant.

Several years ago movie theaters started being built with stadium-style seating and supercomfortable lounge chairs. It was a trend people loved. Who wouldn't? But that left older theaters with conventional seating with a decision to make: jump on board and remodel or save the money and keep the old-fashioned seats. Those that clung to the status quo saw a big reduction in their sales receipts as moviegoers flocked to the newer, more comfortable theaters. It is a wise leader who pays attention to trends even though some of them won't amount to much. The ones that do, the trends that fundamentally change the industry, could make you or break you, depending on whether or not you're on board.

It is natural to resist change. When we find ourselves in a comfortable situation, we want to hunker down and stay there. But leadership is about growing and getting better. As E. H. Carr said, "Change is certain. Progress is not." Progress happens when change is embraced and the status quo is recognized for what it is: one of your biggest enemies.

Why Leaders Are Afraid to Rock the Boat

So why are leaders afraid to rock the boat? There's more to it than just a love of the comfortable and the familiar. Here are four more reasons.

Reason #1: The Sacred Cow Syndrome

A sacred cow is an item, an issue, or a practice that has taken on a life of its own. Maybe at one time it was just another thing, but now, with the passage of some years, it has become such a part of the environment that even the mention of doing away with it sends people into fits of anxiety. Of course, some things are iconic and should be held onto. College sports teams, for example, have many traditions that add richness and fun to the school's heritage. But in many businesses, churches, and organizations where progress has ground to a halt, the sacred cows are the problem. They are the cast-in-concrete practices that prevent the business or organization from breathing and stretching and moving forward.

For example, Thom Ranier, who is a church growth expert, has identified some sacred cows commonly found in churches. One is the order of the worship service. Switching it around to make the flow more worshipful, or even just to create a sense of freshness, seems like a good idea, right? Especially since the Bible doesn't say what an order of worship should look like. But many a pastor has met the wrath of his people for changing it. "I just can't worship if we don't say the Lord's Prayer at the beginning of the service. If you don't switch it back to the way it was, I'll have to find someplace else to go to church." Sounds petty, I know. But talk to any pastor and he will tell you he's heard it many times. That's why countless pastors have simply waved the white flag, deciding it just isn't worth it to try to change anything.

Reason #2: The Spooky Legends of Previous Boat-Rockers Who Failed

Every business or organization that has substantial history behind it will have stories about leaders from bygone eras, some who were successful and others who weren't. And sometimes the ones who weren't are more famous. Or at least they are the ones the new leader will hear about first. "Let me tell you about what happened to old so-and-so. Don't do what he did or you won't last very long." More often than not, what the old leader did that got him into trouble was trying to change something.

Here's a point that should be made. In many cases, a small minority of people is able to influence what does or doesn't change. If they are strong-willed, determined, and vocal, they can make themselves seem like a much larger group than they really are. If you're leading and some resistance to your ideas for change flares up, try to determine if the resistance is widespread or just a few people with big mouths. Those active resisters like to pretend they are speaking for everyone, but they almost never are.

Reason #3: What's Being Done Is Working ... Somewhat

"If it ain't broke, don't fix it." We've all heard the adage, and if the subject is car engines or AC units, I would agree. But businesses and organizations are different. They don't have to actually be broken to need some boat-rocking. Even if the product is good, the business model sound, the people well qualified, and the bottom line in the black, the business may be falling short of its potential.

Apple, for example, was a well-established company with 350 projects in development when Steve Jobs became the permanent CEO in 1997. He promptly proceeded to rock the boat by eliminating three hundred projects and focusing on just fifty. He decided the company would quit spreading itself so thin and go whole hog after the next big thing. Suddenly, we were getting iPods and iPhones and iTunes. Not surprisingly, the company's stock was up 9,000 percent. Yet, even with such stories floating around, it can be hard for a leader to pull the trigger on some big, boat-rocking change when a company or organization is well established and working fairly well.

Reason #4: The Change Involves People Who Are Popular

When Whitey Herzog was the manager of the Kansas City Royals, he faced a dilemma with his second baseman, Cookie Rojas. Cookie had been a fine player for the Royals and was beloved by the fans. But age had slowed him down, causing him to become a defensive liability. Whitey also knew he had a hotshot young kid named Frank White waiting in the wings, ready to take over for Cookie. Lesser men would have shied away from making the change because of the potential blowback, but not Whitey. For the good of the team, he made the switch. Many Royals fans wanted to strangle him. They felt he'd been disrespectful to a longtime Royals hero. But history shows it was a great decision, as Frank White became a five-time all-star, an eight-time Gold Glove winner, a World Series champion, and a member of the Royals Hall of Fame.

Personnel changes are often what an organization needs, but they can be the most difficult changes to make, especially if the people involved have made a significant contribution. Some leaders have decided just to wait and let the person retire, which can be a viable option if time is on your side. When it isn't and you have to go ahead and pull the trigger, criticism will come just as surely as the rooster crows at dawn.

As you can see, it's easy to come up with reasons not to rock the boat. One thing that will help you overcome them is to understand that there is a right way and a wrong way to go about making a change. As is the case with most hazardous endeavors, from skydiving to mountain climbing, when done right, the risks go way down.

How to Rock the Boat without Sinking It

Here are seven suggestions that will help you rock your boat without capsizing it.

Suggestion #1: Think Systems, Not People

When a change is needed, the absolute worst thing you can do is try to change people. People haven't changed since the beginning of time, and they're not going to. After thousands of years, we still have the same desires, hopes, fears, and weaknesses. Trends and technologies change all around us, but the essential nature of mankind doesn't. Have you ever heard someone say, "Only the names and faces change"? This is what they're talking about.

So when you look at your business or organization and see that something needs to change, think systems, not people. What can you do to your systems and procedures that will draw more fully on your people's ability? In sports we call it maximizing a player's potential. Don't ask him to be anything other than what he is, but create a strategy that will best utilize his skill set.

> When you look at your business or organization and see that something needs to change, think systems, not people. What can you do to your systems and procedures that will draw more fully on your people's ability?

That's not to say you can't hire specialized people or let some go if they are compromising the team's chance for success. Personnel adjustments are always going to be needed from time to time. But you can't fire your whole company every time you want to change something. And even if you did, only the names and faces would change. You have to design a system—or make adjustments to your current system—that will give you a better chance at success.

Suggestion #2: Think People, Not Robots

When you decide to make a substantive change, to really rock the boat, your people will react. A few might love the idea, but I'm guessing the majority won't. It's human nature. Many of your people will feel disrupted, apprehensive, or downright angry. If they were robots, you could just reprogram them and be done with it. No muss, no fuss. But because they're people, you have to get them on board.

The best way to do that is to sell them on the benefits of the change. Instead of dwelling on all the things that will be different, focus on why the new approach will be better. Really, this is the key to selling everything from dishwashing detergent to automobiles. People must be able to see the benefits they will enjoy. And by the way, if there are no benefits for you to sell to your people, if all the benefits are for you and none are for them, then don't make the change. If you do, it will be met with apathy at best and opposition at worst. Either way, it will be a step backward. Robots may be complicated, with their circuit boards and software, but people aren't. Be good to them and they will be good to you.

Suggestion #3: Show Respect to Past Forms and Methods

When you're selling your ideas for change to your people, there's nothing to be gained by trashing what has gone before, but there's plenty to be lost. Whatever the forms and methods are that you're changing, they were put into place by somebody who, even if he or she is gone, may still have friends in the company. Why risk alienating those people by disrespecting the work their friend did? It just isn't necessary.

This is a mistake commonly made by aggressive young leaders who are trying to be "cutting edge" and are desperate to sever ties with the past. For example, a young, hip worship leader coming into a church gains nothing by trashing the traditional music that his predecessor favored. Both styles have their place and are enjoyed by many people; there's just no reason to disrespect either one. Even if he wants to completely do away with all traditional music, the new guy should speak well of the past and simply explain why a new approach is needed.

Suggestion #4: Get Input

Have you noticed that almost every business now uses customer surveys? Look at your receipt the next time you eat out at a chain restaurant. Chances are there will be instructions at the bottom for how you can answer a few questions and get a free appetizer. Leaders make a terrible mistake when they fail to get input from their employees and customers. Who knows better what your strengths and weaknesses are than the people you serve and who serve you?

I like how many companies will test a new product or service in a limited area and for a limited time before they dive in headfirst and push it nationwide. I'm sure McDonald's wishes it had done that in 1996 before spending $150 million on an ad campaign for its Arch Deluxe sandwich. The burger flopped because, well, people just didn't like it, a fact that could have been ascertained if the company had just asked for some input.

Suggestion #5: Get Your Influencers on Board

In every business or organization, there are key players—influencers—who have been around a while and earned a lot of trust. If those people are in your corner and will endorse the changes you have in mind, you have taken a huge step forward. I suggest that you meet with your influencers first, perhaps even one-on-one, to explain your idea and why you think it will help your company or organization. But be ready! These influencers will likely be sharp people who have been around a while. To paraphrase the Farmers Insurance commercial, "They know a thing or two because they've seen a thing or two." They may well ask you some hard questions about your proposed change. Don't be afraid of that. Those questions will test and likely refine your idea. (See Suggestion #4.)

Suggestion #6: Make the Change a Process Rather Than an Event

When you were a kid, you probably didn't go from riding a tricycle to riding a bicycle in one day. I'm guessing the move was made gradually and that training wheels were involved. Maybe a parent or an older sibling ran along beside you for a while to make sure you didn't fall over.

Likewise, don't just circle a day on the calendar and say, "This is when everything will be different." Instead, bring people along gradually. If new procedures are being put into place or if people are being promoted into new positions, offer training and support that starts before the change date and continues afterward. And don't overreact to mistakes. Give people a chance to settle in and get comfortable with the new approach. Remember, Rome wasn't built in a day.

Suggestion #7: Measure and Evaluate the Success of Your Changes

Obviously, you wouldn't make a change unless you believed it would help your business or organization. But the list of leaders who overestimated the success of their big new idea is long. For example, in 1982 Colgate, the toothpaste company, started making and selling frozen dinners. I guess at the time it seemed like a good idea. But the idea flopped so spectacularly that not only did the frozen dinners not sell, the company's toothpaste products, which were their bread and butter (no pun intended), started tanking too. People said the lasagna tasted like toothpaste and the toothpaste tasted like lasagna, which probably wasn't actually true, but you can understand how the idea could get into people's heads.

On paper an idea might seem like a surefire winner. That doesn't mean it will be, however. You need to monitor things very carefully and make sure your changes aren't doing more harm than good.

When I think about change, I'm reminded of a story about Albert Einstein. After he gave a test to his physics students at Princeton, one of them stopped him in the hallway and said, "Dr. Einstein, wasn't that the same exam you gave to this physics class last year?"

Einstein nodded and admitted that it was.

The student said, "But why? Aren't you afraid somebody will use last year's answers to cheat on the test?"

Einstein smiled and said, "No, I'm not afraid at all. You see, just since last year our understanding of physics has expanded so much that none of last year's answers are still correct."

Change is happening all around us. Rather than shrinking or hiding from it, we need to get in on it. It was H. G. Wells who said, "Adapt or perish, now as ever, is nature's inexorable imperative."

Go ahead. Rock that boat.

CHAPTER 7

Reluctant to Live with Stress

I know a little bit about stress.

As an NBA general manager, I felt enormous stress, especially when draft time came around. To compete in big-time professional sports—especially the NBA, because rosters are so small—you simply cannot afford to miss on your draft picks. If you miss and your archrival strikes gold, it can tip the balance of power drastically, and your team might take years to recover.

In 1970, my first year as GM of the Chicago Bulls, we had the eleventh pick. We did our homework and settled on Jimmy Collins out of New Mexico State. It felt like the right pick, and we had high hopes. Unfortunately, Jimmy never became the player we envisioned. That's bad enough, but what made matters worse was that there had been two players available who were eventually inducted into the NBA Hall of Fame: Nate Archibald and Calvin Murphy. We could have had either one of them.

And then there was 1993, the year the Orlando Magic had the first pick in the draft and selected Chris Webber, a member of Michigan's famous "Fab Five." Chris, though only a sophomore, was one of the most decorated college basketball players in America. The fans loved our choice. So what did I do? I immediately traded him to the Golden State Warriors for Penny Hardaway and three first-round draft picks. Penny was not as celebrated as Chris and went to a "mid-major" school rather than having a Big Ten pedigree like Chris. It would be an understatement to say this trade was not embraced by our fans. I bet Al Capone was more popular with FBI agents than I was with Magic fans.

I believed Penny, a six-seven point guard, was an extraordinary talent. But at the time the stress was excruciating as I wondered if I had made a brilliant move or a moronic one. Only time would tell. Almost daily I pleaded with God to please let Penny be as good as I believed he was. If he'd been a bust compared to Chris Webber, who turned out to be an all-star, I may have been hung from the flagpole outside our arena. Thankfully, Penny was an all-star himself, truly a magnificent player. Today, most people in Orlando love Penny so much they've forgotten we even drafted Chris Webber.

But it wasn't just the drafts.

In all the years I worked as an NBA executive, I have never had a designated seat. I have always stood during the games. It's a nerves thing. I feel so wired that I can't relax. Even when the team is on the road, I find it too nerve-racking to listen to the game on the radio or to sit and watch in my home. I generally tune in at the end to find out what happened and spare myself all that extra stress.

When you're in leadership, you have stress. That's just the way it is.

Sometimes it comes from a tough boss. Remember George Steinbrenner, the owner of the New York Yankees? He owned the team for thirty-seven years and gained a reputation as one of the toughest bosses in sports. During a twenty-two-year period of his ownership, he had twenty-one managers. I wonder if the guys even bothered to set up their offices.

But even if you don't have a tough boss, there are other ways stress can worm its way into your life through your leadership role. Your workload will likely be greater than it would be if you weren't in leadership. You will surely have to concern yourself with problem employees from time to time and be responsible for managing large amounts of money wisely, maybe in a bad economy. You could have to contend with expectations from higher-ups that you feel are unreasonable. If you're a new leader, you may be asked to come in and clean up someone else's mess. If you're an older leader, you may be expected to adapt your organization to changing trends and technologies. And none of this takes into account the pressure you may put on yourself to do a great job. Add it all together and one thing becomes clear: leadership is stressful!

I wouldn't blame anyone for being reluctant to take on a leadership role out of concerns about stress. In fact, I will say that you *shouldn't* accept a leadership role if you're not emotionally healthy.

I wouldn't blame anyone for being reluctant to take on a leadership role out of concerns about stress. In fact, I will say that you *shouldn't* accept a leadership role if you're not emotionally healthy. If you're not functioning well at home or in your marriage, it would be unwise for you to take on even more stress. Instead, find something to do that doesn't bring a lot of pressure into your life and use that time to get your head and heart together.

However, if you *are* emotionally healthy, there's no reason to be afraid of leadership stress. The key is knowing how (and how *not*) to handle it.

Bad Stress Relievers

Sometimes you have to blast before you can build. You have to blow up the old building and clear away the rubble before you can start to build something new. That is certainly true when dealing with stress. The following bad stress relievers are techniques and habits that may make you feel better in the moment but are no doubt hurting you in the long run. You need to blow them up and get them out of your life so you can start to develop new, more positive techniques.

Bad Stress Reliever #1: Angry Outbursts

There have been a lot of hotheads in professional sports, but Billy Martin may have been the grand champion of them all during his days as manager of the Yankees. On June 4, 1988, the *Los Angeles Times* carried a headline that read, "Martin Gets Warned by Umpires: AL Crew Chiefs Say Further Outbursts Won't Be Tolerated." This was in the aftermath of Billy throwing dirt on umpire Dale Scott when the Yankees were playing in Oakland. He got a three-game suspension and a $1,000 fine. Of course, this had little, if any, impact on his conduct. Billy Martin was always a powder keg waiting to explode, no matter how much he was fined or warned.

People with short fuses love to say, "I can't help it. All that emotion has to go someplace. I'm just letting it out, blowing off steam. If I didn't, I'd probably have a heart attack." But is this true? There's plenty of medical research that confirms the negative effects of uncontrolled anger on the body. High blood pressure, headaches, gastrointestinal issues, ulcers, hives, respiratory distress, and even diarrhea are known to be caused or made worse by angry outbursts. Any effort to portray habitual explosions of anger as a kind of health benefit is just silly.

But it isn't just the damage we do to ourselves that matters; it's also the damage our angry outbursts to do the people around us. How many children are there who cower in fear when a parent comes home after a bad day at the office? How many wives walk on eggshells around volatile husbands that perceive every little misstep as a personal attack? How many employees try their best to avoid bosses who never seem to be happy with anything they do? Uncontrolled anger causes terror, pure and simple.

It also causes physical injury and death.

It is common to attribute explosive, violent crime to mental illness. But Paolo del Vecchio of the Substance Abuse and Mental Health Services Administration disagrees. He said, "Violence by those with mental illness is so small that even if you could somehow cure it all, 95 percent of violent crime would still exist."[12]

So who commits most of the violent crimes in America today? Not mentally ill people but rather angry people. The *Washington Post* reports that roughly twenty-two million Americans have impulsive anger issues.[13] They shout hateful words, break things, and throw punches when circumstances don't go their way. And yes, people get hurt, especially young people. Wright State University found that

---

12 Laura L. Hayes, "How to Stop Violence: Mentally Ill People Aren't Killers. Angry People Are," Slate, April 9, 2014, https://slate.com/technology/2014/04/anger-causes-violence-treat-it-rather-than-mental-illness-to-stop-mass-murder.html.

13 Christopher Ingraham, "Nearly 1 in 10 Americans Have Severe Anger Issues and Access to Guns, *Washington Post* online, April 8, 2015, https://www.washingtonpost.com/news/wonk/wp/2015/04/08/nearly-1-in-10-americans-have-severe-anger-issues-and-access-to-guns/.

people between the ages of twelve and twenty-four are the most likely to be the victims of violent outbursts.[14] This makes sense when you think about young people being less able to protect themselves from a rampaging adult or being trapped in the home and having no place to go to escape the violence.

It is truly twisted thinking that insists on seeing explosive anger as a therapeutic exercise. It may sound good to talk about "blowing off steam," but the reality is far more frightening and destructive.

Bad Stress Reliever #2: Alcohol or Drugs

How many times have you seen the protagonist in a Hollywood movie turn to the wet bar and pour himself a drink in a moment of extreme stress? He knocks it back and grimaces as it goes down, then pours another. And then maybe another. The message is clear: *Our hero needs alcohol if he's going to make it through this dire situation.*

Or perhaps you know someone who uses alcohol as a stress reliever. "I just need it to take the edge off," he'll often say. "It calms me," she'll explain.

And then of course there's marijuana. "Mellow" is a word that's often used to describe someone who's smoking weed, often accompanied by the image of a semidazed person kicking back in a state of foggy euphoria. Now that marijuana is being legalized across the country, countless promotional campaigns tout it as the ultimate treatment for anxiety. But the buyer should beware. Marijuana, like alcohol, may put you in a temporary daze, but it does nothing to address the real cause of your stress. Whenever you come down from

---

14 "Warning Signs of Violence," Wright State University, posted October 2, 2014, https://www.wright.edu/student-affairs/health-and-wellness/counseling-and-wellness/workshops-and-self-help/article/warning-signs-of-violence.

your high or sober up from your binge, your problems are right there waiting for you.

And think about the daze that marijuana puts you in. Reports are coming out of states where marijuana has been legalized, and they're not encouraging. Traffic accidents are up considerably, the result of people driving while high.[15] Whatever stress you may think your weed is saving you from, you risk other problems that could raise your stress level exponentially.

Bad Stress Reliever #3: Food

It has long been known that a powerful connection exists between stress and weight gain. It has to do with a hormone called cortisol. Persistent stress causes the adrenal glands to release it into the body, and it, in turn, increases the appetite. Suddenly, you just have to eat, and the heavier and richer the food is, the better you feel. Hence the term "comfort food." Those gravy-smothered biscuits with that big slab of meatloaf make the world look so much better.

By the way, research shows that overeating to relieve stress is more of a female thing than a male thing. Perhaps because of cultural stereotypes or expectations, men are more likely to reach for a cigarette or a bottle when they become stressed, while women will make another trip to the refrigerator. Karen Scalf Linamen captured this truth in the title of her book, *Just Hand Over the Chocolate and No One Will Get Hurt*.

Sadly, the weight gain that results from stress eating only gives the person yet another reason to feel stressed. The growing number of items in your closet that no longer fit, the horrifying glance at the mirror when you step out of the shower, and the sudden difficulty

15 Jen Christensen, "States That Legalized Recreational Weed See Increase in Car Accidents, Studies Say," CNN, October 18, 2018, https://www.cnn.com/2018/10/18/health/marijuana-driving-accidents-bn/index.html.

you have clipping your toenails or tying your shoes can fill you with self-loathing. Even then, when stress kicks in, your stomach will start growling if you don't train it not to.

Bad Stress Reliever #4: Promiscuity

Sex with guardrails—that is, within the marriage relationship—is a great stress reducer. Physically, it releases hormones and endorphins that elevate mood. Emotionally, it contributes to intimacy, which is at the heart of every great marriage. On the other hand, sex without guardrails—called promiscuity—can be exciting in the moment but often leaves emotional wreckage in its wake.

In our generation it's fashionable to talk about "friends with benefits" or "casual" sex with "no strings attached." The terms themselves are light and airy, suggesting the kind of carefree, let's-have-a-good-time lifestyle that is high fun and low stress. In truth, promiscuous people are not as happy as advertised. They usually experience fleeting moments of pleasure followed by long periods of emptiness and, yes, loneliness. And that's if they're fortunate enough not to get emotionally entangled with some *Fatal Attraction*–, possessive-, psycho-type who didn't read the fine print about the "no strings" part of the deal.

Sadly, the four bad stress relievers I've just mentioned are seen as "good" by many people. That's because our culture, with its upside-down values, puts its stamp of approval on blowing off steam, hitting the bars, stuffing oneself, and having recreational sex. Thousands of movies, TV episodes, and novels are released every year that depict these behaviors as being perfectly normal, even admirable. Imagine people's confusion and disillusionment when they wake up one day—as many of them do—and realize that they were sold a bill of goods—

that all the things that were supposed to lower their stress and make them happy actually had the opposite effect.

You can avoid having a moment like that.

Good Stress Relievers

Let's start with the most obvious ones and work toward the less obvious ones. But remember, just because something is obvious doesn't mean you have thought about it. People overlook or neglect the obvious all the time, like the motorcyclist who's speeding down the highway with his helmet strapped to the back of his bike. I learned a long time ago never to assume that people will grasp the obvious.

Good Stress Reliever #1: Time Off

You've heard the saying: "All work and no play makes Jack a dull boy."

It also makes Jack a tired boy.

And a grouchy boy.

And a less productive boy.

Forward-thinking companies are recognizing this and offering remedies like shorter work weeks, more vacation time, in-house workout facilities, basketball courts on site, and daycare service for employees with kids so they don't have to add to their work day by running all over creation fighting traffic to drop off and pick up their children. If you're not fortunate enough to work for such a company, you'll need to find your own ways of getting away from the workplace grind.

Let me encourage you to be strong on this point. In our dog-eat-dog world, there's always the temptation to knock yourself out. You justify it by reminding yourself that there's an example to be set for your employees and bonuses and promotions to be earned from your superiors. But it's a trap! While you tell yourself you're working hard now to enjoy the fruits of your labor later, you will likely find that those fruits always seem to be sitting out there on the horizon, close enough to be tantalizing but never quite close enough to reach. This is what happens to many people. They tell themselves the heavy workload is only temporary. Then suddenly they realize that years have gone by and they're still locked into the same old grind.

Time off doesn't just happen. You have to be intentional about it. And keep in mind that a vacation doesn't have to be days long. A vacation could be a single afternoon or even an hour out of your day. Get up from your desk on a pretty day and walk around the block a couple of times. Soak up some sunshine and listen to the music of the birds in the trees. Any time you spend clearing your head and relaxing helps.

Good Stress Reliever #2: Capable Team Members

Let's be honest. Lots of people in leadership, especially in smaller companies or organizations, spend way too much time cleaning up the messes of subordinates who aren't cutting it, serving as a counselor for employees who have personal problems, or troubleshooting situations that team leaders ought to be able to handle on their own. To a degree, leaders need to be "hands on" with their people, but high-maintenance, less-than-competent employees can add lots of unnecessary stress to a leader's life.

This problem can be kept to a minimum by being careful whom you allow on your team. The old adage "An ounce of prevention is worth a pound of cure" really is true. Sometimes leaders lower their hiring standards to try to help out a struggling friend or someone they feel sorry for. Such a move may be admirable from a humanitarian standpoint but could add significantly to your stress if the person turns out to be a problem. Make every effort to hire competent, low-maintenance people.

It's also important to provide adequate training and continuing support. A good many employee failures could be avoided if leaders would step up their training and coaching game.

Finally, it's critical to have a system in place that addresses "people problems" before they land in your lap. Yes, the big stuff will eventually work its way up to you, but the smaller issues should be dealt with by others. And yes, it's those smaller things that create so much of our stress. Think of the housefly that's buzzing around your food when you're trying to eat. It's not going to wreck your life, but it sure gets on your nerves.

Now think of two houseflies. Or five. Or ten.

You get the idea.

Good Stress Reliever #3: Exercise

You don't need any highfalutin research to tell you that mental stress produces physical symptoms. Hypertension, headaches, nervousness, dry mouth, sweaty hands, shortness of breath, and gastrointestinal upheavals are just a few of the nasty little gifts stress doles out. Exercise helps by reducing the body's levels of stress hormones, such as adrenaline and cortisol, and releasing endorphins, which are the body's natural pain killers and mood elevators. This is why a stressed-out person at the gym pounding on a heavy bag will always feel better when the workout is over. "I took out my frustrations on that bag!" will likely be the explanation, but there's more to it than that. The body loves exercise and offers lavish benefits and rewards to those who dedicate themselves to it.

If you played sports when you were a kid, your parents probably told you to rest up on game days. "Don't play too hard or you won't have any energy left for the game." By contrast, you'll find most professional athletes working out hard on game day, lifting weights, running sprints, doing agility or shooting drills, taking batting practice, and so on. They know what many parents do not, that activity is the great energizer. If pro athletes lay on the couch all day and then walked onto the field/court at night and tried to play, they would be sluggish and slow.

If you're a leader, your challenge is going to be finding time to exercise. My advice is to do it first thing in the morning. This makes sense for three reasons. One, days rarely develop the way we expect them to. Your plan to exercise later in the day can get derailed by some unexpected turn of events. Two, you're fresher in the morning and can attack your exercise time with more vigor. Later in the day, when you're already tired, you may be tempted to cut your workout short or skip it altogether. And three, starting your day with a workout will energize you for what you have to face. You won't be like so many people who come dragging in to work half asleep, sucking down coffee to try to wake themselves up.

Leadership is an emotional enterprise. You can feel anxious, excited, frustrated, happy, angry, and relieved all in one day.

Good Stress Reliever #4: Emotional Support

Leadership is an emotional enterprise. You can feel anxious, excited, frustrated, happy, angry, and relieved all in one day. In fact, sometimes you can run the gamut of these emotions in a single hour, depending on how fast things move in your company or organization. The good thing about this is that your work is never boring. The bad thing is that it's incredibly draining.

Emotional strain is every bit as draining as physical work, which is why it's important to have good emotional support.

Emotional support is best found in a friend, a confidant. Yes, you can go on social media and vent all your frustrations, and maybe your contacts will chime in and give you lots of likes and emojis. But it's much better if you can sit down with someone and actually talk. A face-to-face conversation can achieve so much greater depth, and nuances like facial expressions and voice inflection help it along. Social media posts, text messages, and emails simply can't achieve what a face-to-face conversation can.

The trick is finding the right person to talk to. Just because you connect well with someone doesn't mean that person will be a good source of emotional support. If, for example, your friend struggles with his own load of emotional baggage, he'll be in no position to help you with yours. There's also the issue of confidentiality. You might love someone to death but know that he can't keep a secret. When you blow off steam to someone, you must be absolutely certain the information will go no further. If you have to worry about confidentiality, that's just one more thing to stress about! And then, finally, it's best to draw your emotional support from someone who is wise. The person doesn't have to be in the same business, or even in business at all, but it's great if the person has good common sense.

Over the years I have heard countless stories about leaders who veered off into decadent behaviors or ran into health problems or became bitter and angry, and I always wonder if part of the reason was a lack of sufficient emotional support. People, especially men, can be very prideful and have an "I can do it by myself" mentality. And maybe some can. But almost everyone benefits tremendously from solid emotional support.

Good Stress Reliever #5: A Spiritual Anchor

Have you ever been fishing on a windy day? If so, you know how frustrating it is. You want to toss your lure into that little opening at the edge of the cattails where you know the big bass like to hang out, but before you can cock your wrist and let it fly, the wind has blown you out of range. What do you need? You need an anchor.

Stress is like the wind in that it will blow you off course spiritually. Highly stressed people often wake up one day and realize that they are not where they used to be in terms of their walk with God. They may have allowed their personal self-discipline to slip. Maybe anger and salty language have become the norm. Perhaps what was once regular church attendance has become sporadic at best. Maybe what used to be a caring attitude toward struggling, high-maintenance employees has turned to cynicism. You don't get to such a place overnight. It happens gradually as stress becomes more and more a part of your life.

That's why you need an anchor. An anchor will keep you from being blown all over the place. Hebrews 6:19 says, "This hope is a strong and trustworthy anchor for our souls." What hope is he talking about? If you read the entire passage, it's clear that he's talking about God's promises. Leaders who want to remain steady and strong spiritually must be able to lift their eyes above the fray and look beyond the headaches and challenges of the daily grind to what God has in store. In my years as a leader at just about every level, I survived by reminding myself that whatever hardship or difficulty I was dealing with at the moment was only temporary, that God had made promises to me that transcended whatever I happened to be struggling with. Colossians 3:1–2 says, "Since you have been raised to new life with Christ, set your sights on the realities of heaven, where Christ sits in the place of honor at God's right hand. Think about the things of heaven, not the things of earth." That's the single best piece of advice I could give to someone who is being blown all over the place by the howling winds of stress. Let God's promises be your anchor.

Of course, this presupposes that you know what God's promises are. The anchor can't work for you if you forget and leave it on shore. That's why I challenge you to make sure you spend time with the Word of God. Don't let the fact that you are busy be an excuse. Take a few minutes each day and let God speak to you through the Bible. You'll find it astonishing how often what you read will relate specifically to what you're dealing with.

To wrap up this chapter, I'll share a story about Dwight D. Eisenhower that I love.

In 1955 he was invited to give the commencement address at Penn State University, where his brother, Milton, was the president. When the day arrived, the skies were cloudy and the weather forecast iffy. Ike was asked if he would prefer to have the ceremony indoors to avoid the possibility of getting wet. He shrugged and said, "You decide. I haven't worried about the weather since June 6, 1944."

June 6, 1944 was D-Day, the day the allied forces, under General Eisenhower's leadership, invaded northern France by landing on the beach at Normandy. Obviously, the weather would play a critical role then, and in fact the invasion was originally scheduled for June 4 but had to be postponed because of high winds and heavy seas. The man who would eventually become our thirty-fourth president learned through that experience that stressing out about something doesn't change a thing. It's better to stay calm and adjust to whatever happens.

You may never be called upon to lead an invasion that will tip the balance of world power, but whatever your leadership challenge is, the techniques I've just shared will help you stay calm and be a stabilizing influence for your entire team.

CHAPTER 8

Reluctant to Fail

I have achieved some success as a leader. Others can judge how much, but as I look back on my life, I'm pretty amazed at the jobs I've held, the people I've met, and the victories I've been privileged to be a part of. That is not to say there weren't some embarrassing moments along the way. This chapter is about failure, and I have had some doozies.

At the beginning of the last chapter, I told you about the time I left two future Hall of Fame players on the NBA draft board and took a player that ended up playing seventy-four total NBA games and averaging 3.8 points a game. As failures go, that one was pretty spectacular. But it is by no means the only one in my portfolio.

During the 1973–1974 NBA season, I was in my first year as the general manager of the Atlanta Hawks. The team wasn't very good and wasn't drawing many fans, so I decided to pull out all the stops and line up some great promotions. About that time I heard of a trained pig act—yes, I said a trained pig act—called Uncle Heavy and His Pork Chop Review. I booked them to do a halftime show at one of our Saturday night games.

I was pretty proud of myself. After all, doesn't everyone love an animal act? Well, I can tell you one person who *didn't* love it: our team president, John Wilcox. On Monday morning I was summoned to his office and received what was quite possibly the most thorough chewing out of my career. John was at the game with some of his cultured friends and was aghast at the sight of pigs rooting and snorting as they ran around on the floor. He called it humiliating to watch. I remember slinking out of his office and thinking of a cartoon that once appeared in a leadership magazine. It showed a Dilbert-like character with no rear end. It was as if a monster had bitten his backside clean off and left nothing but jagged teeth marks where his posterior should be. The caption said, "I just got back from having a little chat with the boss."

But some time passed and softened the blow, as it always does, and the next year I found myself working for the Philadelphia 76ers. Again I was in charge of halftime shows, and again I heard about Uncle Heavy and his trained pig act. Only now it was Uncle Heavy and His Pork Chop Review, featuring Pepper the Singing Pig. Even in spite of my previous disastrous results with this act, I simply couldn't resist. Surely Philadelphians would love a singing pig!

Wrong.

The show was okay until it came time for Pepper to sing. Of course, "sing" is a bit of a stretch. Pepper didn't actually sing. Uncle Heavy would hold a microphone up to Pepper's snout and then put his arm around him and poke him in a way that was not noticeable to the audience. This, of course, caused Pepper to squeal. Who among us *wouldn't* squeal if we were being repeatedly poked? But squealing wasn't good enough for the Philly fans. They wanted some honest-to-goodness singing and began to let their feelings be known with a chorus of lusty boos.

Well, pigs have feelings too. And in Pepper's case, possibly some gastrointestinal problems. At any rate, Pepper's response to the crowd's displeasure was to produce a sizable contribution from his opposite end that sent the arena custodians scrambling for shovels and mops and buckets. The audience howled, of course, and likely wondered what kind of idiot books a trained pig routine for a basketball game halftime show.

I, of course, was that kind of idiot. I had done it not once but twice, to disastrous results both times. By the way, that was the end of my association with Uncle Heavy and his pigs. I'm not saying it has stuck with me, but I do break out into a cold sweat when I see someone eating a ham sandwich.

This much I know: all leaders fail. Name the greatest leader you can think of, and I promise you'll be able to dig into his or her past and find a Pepper the Singing Pig. Or two. Or three.

Abraham Lincoln, for example, is one of our greatest presidents, but he was no stranger to failure. He suffered bankruptcy, broken family relationships, and a long string of political defeats and humiliations. A few months before he was nominated for president, the Philadelphia *Press* ran an article about the upcoming nominating convention that included a list of forty-five possible candidates. Lincoln had suffered so many failures that his name didn't even appear on the list. One newspaper editor wrote: "The Hon. Abe Lincoln is undoubtedly the most unfortunate politician that has ever attempted to rise in Illinois. In everything he undertakes, politically, he seems doomed to failure."[16]

History makes it clear. Leadership and failure go together.

---

16 Gene Griessman and Pat Williams, *Lincoln Speaks to Leaders* (Charleston: Advantage Media, 2009), 100.

For that reason, I totally understand if you're reluctant to step into a leadership role. I get that you don't want to let people down. You don't want to embarrass yourself. You don't want to set your company or organization back by making bad decisions. Those are honorable feelings. But here's what you must remember: *anybody* who steps into the leadership role that is currently beckoning you is going to produce some failures. If you think that by refusing to accept the role you are sparing your company or organization the indignity of failure, you're wrong. *Any* leader who steps into the role and stays for a significant amount of time is going to fail.

The way to think about failure is not to let it scare you into a full-scale retreat but to accept that it's going to happen and then begin to prepare yourself in such a way that it doesn't happen often.

The way to think about failure is not to let it scare you into a full-scale retreat but to accept that it's going to happen and then begin to prepare yourself in such a way that it doesn't happen often.

Minimizing Failure

One of the great things technology has done for us in recent years is make it possible for us to better protect our homes. Especially popular are the video doorbells that are connected to our cell phones. They enable us to see and speak to whoever is at our door even when we're not at home. This, of course, doesn't mean your home will never be broken into, but it does reduce the probability.

Likewise, when it comes to leadership, there's no way to guarantee that you'll never fail, but you can sure take steps to minimize failure. Here are some strategies that will help.

Strategy #1: Get Organized

How many failures have happened simply because something important was forgotten or misplaced? My cowriter and friend, Mark Atteberry, tells about the time he was sleeping in on a Saturday morning. Out of a deep sleep, he heard his phone ring and groggily groped for it on the bedside table. The conversation went like this:

Mark: Hello?

Caller: Hey, Mark, where are you? Are you on your way?

Mark: Huh? Who is this?

Caller: This is Joe. We're all here at the prayer breakfast waiting on you. You're supposed to speak this morning. Remember?

He hadn't remembered.

Mark will tell you that was the day he got more organized. He completely changed the way he booked engagements and kept his schedule. Specifically, he entrusted that part of his life to someone else, someone who was much better at managing such details. And guess what? He's never had an embarrassing moment like that since.

Lots of disorganized people will say they like to fly by the seat of their pants. "I do my best work when I just go with the flow," they say. Translation: "I work better when I don't prepare ahead of time and just make it up as I go along."

Or they say, "I work better under pressure." Translation: "I work better when I'm behind and scrambling to get my work done on time."

I will admit that there's more than one way to approach work. But I believe it's an indisputable fact that people who are disorganized and constantly scrambling to get things done at the last minute will experience more embarrassments and failures than people who are organized and prepared.

Strategy #2: Delegate

I talked about this in chapter two, but it's worth hitting again here because people who resist delegating are often highly organized. In fact, the *reason* they resist delegating is *because* they are highly organized. They love to justify their refusal to delegate by puffing up their chests and talking about how they have everything under control. But people who like to brag about having everything under control are usually micromanagers, and micromanagers are generally not effective leaders, mostly because they spread themselves too thin. They juggle too many responsibilities. They feel like they have to be involved in every decision instead of trusting people who are more gifted than they are.

Case in point: Jimmy Carter, our thirty-ninth president. He was a legendary micromanager. Trained as a nuclear engineer, he had the kind of mind that thrived on detail, which made him think he could run everything himself. And he did, but not well. His term in office was marked by gas shortages, a 14 percent inflation rate, and the Iranian hostage crisis. Almost no one thinks of Jimmy Carter as one of our better presidents.

By contrast, Ronald Reagan, Carter's successor, was a big picture guy who put other people in charge of the details. Reagan was often teased for reading summaries prepared by subordinates, selecting an option from a list of choices, and then taking a nap. It's fair to say that Jimmy Carter was more intellectually gifted than Ronald Reagan and just as well-intentioned, but Reagan is judged by history to be the better president in large part because he delegated a lot of work to gifted people and allowed them to use their expertise.

In your role as a leader, you'll increase your chances of succeeding exponentially if you delegate to capable people. The key word is "capable." Delegation only works if you choose people who can get the job done. If you don't have them, find them.

Strategy #3: Keep Learning

Historians have determined the following:

Between the years 1500 and 1830, human knowledge doubled.

Between 1830 and 1930, it doubled again.

Today human knowledge doubles every fifteen to seventeen months.

What does this mean? It means that what you know now may be enough for today, but it won't be enough for tomorrow. One of the great things about living in this generation is that we have so much information at our fingertips. Hopping on the internet to find a piece of information is a thousand times easier than getting into your car and driving to the library and digging through musty old books for an hour or two. Shooting someone an email is a thousand times easier than writing an actual letter, stamping it, and mailing it. If you could resurrect a great leader who died in the 1930s and drop him into our world today, he would find it unrecognizable. He might think he was on another planet! Even someone from the 1970s would look at the technology we routinely use today and not know what half the devices we use are, let alone how to use them.

Here's a simple truth: things are changing so quickly that if you're not continually learning, you're falling behind because somewhere out there one or more of your competitors *is* studying and learning and expanding his or her capabilities. Henry Wadsworth Longfellow had it right when he wrote, "The heights by great men reached and kept were not attained by sudden flight, but they, while their companions slept, were toiling upward in the night."

I strongly recommend that you avail yourself of conferences and seminars, but more than anything, I encourage you to read. The fact that you're reading this book is a sign that you know reading is important. But do you realize how important? If you read the right five books on any one subject, you can consider yourself a globally leading authority on that subject.

Consider that for a moment.

You can choose any subject that interests you. If you read five books on that subject, you will know more about that subject that the vast majority of people in the world. You will actually be an expert. Then consider that if you read just one hour a day, you can read a book a week. That means that in just five weeks you can become an expert on any subject you choose. This is the kind of attitude that will not only keep you up with your competition but also put you ahead.

Strategy #4: Stay Flexible

Abraham Lincoln once said, "You must lead a country the way you would steer a riverboat. You don't just set your compass and head south, or you will quickly run aground. Instead, you steer from point to point according to how the river is running and the obstacles that appear in your path."

Think about a basketball coach. He never says to his players, "Okay, we're going to start out in a man-to-man defense, then after ten minutes we'll switch to a two-one-two zone. Then after five minutes of zone, we'll go to a box-and-one." Such a plan would be ridiculous because it would fail to take into consideration the flow of the game. What if the man-to-man defense is working beautifully? In that case the coach would be crazy to switch to something else. He'd actually be helping the opponent!

Pastors understand the importance of staying flexible. Many of them plan their preaching six months to a year in advance. They can tell you that four months from now they plan to preach a sermon series on a certain subject. But if something unexpected or catastrophic happens that impacts the congregation in the meantime, those plans will change.

There's an old saying that when we make our plans, God laughs. Sometimes it sure seems that way. Wise is the leader who doesn't carve his plans in stone.

Strategy #5: Maintain Your Poise

Have you heard it said that sports teams take on the personality of their coach or manager? It's absolutely true! I've seen it again and again. When you have a leader that is poised and under control, the entire team will be. But if you have a leader who is volatile, who is constantly losing his cool and yelling and screaming, I promise you the entire team will suffer from instability.

Without question, Jesus was the most poised leader who ever lived. Imagine having groups of people who hate you following you around, parsing your every word to try to find the smallest mistake, and asking you questions that are designed to trip you up and make you look foolish. Wouldn't it be hard to take that without going off on an angry rant? But Jesus never did. Day after day the Pharisees set traps for him, and day after day he calmly sidestepped them and kept right on preaching and ministering to people in need. It is no surprise, then, that after he was gone, his disciples (his team), especially Peter and John, showed remarkable poise when they were threatened and proved to be dynamic leaders for the early church. If they had been given to panic and rash, knee-jerk decisions, the history of the church would have no doubt looked very different.

Henry Kissinger once quipped, "Next week there can't be any crisis. My schedule is already full." Oh, how nice it would be if we could schedule our crises and prepare for them! But we can't, so the next best thing is to remain poised and thinking clearly when they come.

Strategy #6: Solicit Ideas

Any leader who has his mind closed to suggestions is going to be a lousy leader. I don't care how smart a leader is, nobody can think of everything. A lot of failures happen, not because something wrong was done, but because there was a better way to do the job that nobody thought of. Many a leader has seen a competitor do something brilliant and said, "Wow, I wish I had thought of that!"

One of my sports management mentors, Bill Veeck, owned the Cleveland Indians, the Saint Louis Browns, and the Chicago White Sox. He told me once that his best ideas came from the fans. For example, he started getting a lot of complaints about concessions and souvenir vendors walking through the stands and blocking the people's view of the game. Somebody mused that he ought to have shorter vendors that didn't get in the way. So what did he do? You guessed it! He hired a team of "short people" to sell his refreshments and souvenirs.

> Leaders sometimes fall into the trap of thinking they know what's best for their customers when in fact it's the customer who knows better than anybody what would make the business even better.

Here's something to remember. The best ideas are likely to come from the people who are living the experience, not the people who are sequestered in some board room puffing on cigars and counting their money. Leaders sometimes fall into the trap of thinking they know what's best for their customers when in fact it's the customer who knows better than anybody what would make the business even better. This is why most successful businesses nowadays solicit your opinions and suggestions every time you do business with them. Conversely, have you noticed that lousy businesses almost never ask for an opinion or a suggestion?

Here's one more thought on the subject of soliciting ideas. If you get a good one, use it! Sometimes leaders hesitate to use a good idea that comes their way for the silliest reasons, like someone else might get the credit or it goes against the grain of the leader's preferred way of doing things. Understand that a great idea is a great idea, no matter whom or where it comes from. And a great idea is often great *because* it goes against the grain of how things are currently being done. Only a foolish leader destined for failure ignores a great idea.

Strategy #7: Love Your People

Have you ever worked for somebody you were a little bit afraid of? Maybe you tensed up when your boss came around. Maybe you loved it when he or she was out of the office for the day because it meant you could relax. Some leaders work hard at creating this type of feeling in their employees. They figure that if the employees are intimidated, they'll be more careful to do everything just right.

Sounds reasonable, doesn't it?

The problem is, people don't perform their best when they're scared of messing up. They tend to always play it safe, to always choose the option that is least likely to rock the boat (which is often *not* the best option). Even worse, they turn into "yes people," automatically telling the boss whatever they think he wants to hear instead of daring to disagree or to offer a suggestion that might make things better. There's also the issue of morale. When leaders intimidate their employees, there will be a depressed atmosphere all around. No one will look forward to coming to work.

I encourage you to love your people instead. Some will read the word "love" and think immediately of mushy sentimentality, but that's not what I'm referring to. I'm talking about treating your employees like people instead of automatons that are programmed to do your bidding. Get to know them. Take an interest in their families. Smile and greet them warmly when you walk into the room. Let them know your door is always open and that they can talk to you about anything. Fight for them when they need an advocate.

How does this help you avoid failure? First, it will help you avoid becoming a failure as a human being. But beyond that, it will also ensure that your people will be ready to fight for you. They will want you to succeed because they won't want you to leave. Believe me, there have been many situations where the employees gave less than their best effort because they *wanted* the leader to fail and get fired. In sports this is what is being referred to when you hear someone say that the players "quit" on the coach. They didn't literally quit, but they started giving less than their best effort because they wanted him or her gone.

Processing Failure

If you follow the strategies I just gave you, you won't be failing very often, but you will still fail occasionally. Let's face it—we live in an imperfect world where the best-laid plans of men often go awry. So let me close this chapter by telling you how to process a failure in four simple steps. (Notice I didn't say four "easy" steps.)

Step #1: Identify What Went Wrong

Did you mess up? Did somebody else?

Guess what.

Sometimes in analyzing a failure you'll discover that *nobody* messed up.

That's right. Sometimes a failure is nobody's fault. Sometimes you make the best decision you can based on the information you have and it just doesn't work. Maybe the timing wasn't quite right or the economy tanked shortly after you launched. In politics polls are often used to plot strategy, but sometimes the polls are mistaken. Failure is sometimes inexplicable. Your job is to figure out what, if anything, went wrong. That's the best way to ensure that it doesn't happen again.

Step #2: Make Needed Adjustments

The definition of insanity is to keep doing the same thing over and over while expecting a different result. When life hands you a failure, chances are it will be time to change some things, or at least make some tweaks. Even if you determine that the failure was nobody's fault, you might still learn something from it that will help you position yourself better for the next leg of the journey.

And keep this in mind about making adjustments: sometimes they can be beneficial even when you haven't experienced a failure. Believe me, when the professional sports teams I worked for were good, I never sat back and thought, "We've done everything just right. There's nothing more for me to do." No, no, no! There's always room for improvement. I never stopped trying to think of ways to make us better.

Step #3: Keep in Mind Your Lessons Learned

A Central Florida pastor's wife was her husband's biggest supporter. She was also the person who held him accountable. Anytime a problem blew up in his face, she would be an awesome wife and offer tons of comfort and encouragement. But when the dust settled and the crisis passed, she would take off her wife hat and put on her accountability partner hat and say the same thing every time: "Okay now, what did you learn from this experience?" And she would press her husband until he could articulate his lessons learned.

People assume failures are bad, but they can actually be very, very good. There are millions of people whose lives and careers were made because a failure taught them just the thing they needed to know going forward. We call it "the school of hard knocks." I don't think there's ever been a college that taught more important truths.

Step #4: Let It Go

This is the hardest step for some people. They can't stop thinking about what might have been. Or they can't stop fuming about some injustice they suffered. Or they can't stop thinking about how they were let down by others.

There are two reasons why dragging a failure around with you is the wrong thing to do. First, it will eventually become who you are. It will so permeate your mind and your feelings and your conversations that people will begin to identify you with that failure. "He never got over it" is a phrase people often use in reference to a person like this.

And second, it will drain the sense of risk and adventure right out of you, virtually ensuring that you will never achieve great success. A person who doesn't let go of his failure will make every decision with that failure in mind. Every choice will be the safe choice. Every path followed will be the path of least resistance, the result being mediocrity rather than greatness.

I've never seen a person walking around with a literal ball and chain strapped to his ankle, but I have known people who allowed their failure to act like a ball and chain. I'm talking about smart people with great potential. Don't be one of them. Let your failure go and move on.

The *Reader's Digest* carried a story about a man who wanted to paint his house. The old paint was a problem, and the idea of scraping and sanding just wasn't appealing, so he decided to use a blowtorch and burn the old paint off. As he set up his equipment, he was congratulating himself for being so clever. When the fire department arrived a short time later to pour water on his burning home, that feeling of cleverness had completely disappeared.

Sometimes we can go from feeling really smart to really dumb in minutes. This is the nature of life in an imperfect world. Don't let the possibility of failure keep you from tapping into your leadership skills. You won't be the first person who failed, and you won't be the last. And your failure just might be the key to your eventual success.

CHAPTER 9

Reluctant to Take the Heat

The first day of spring training marks the end of a long winter and puts a smile on the faces of baseball fans. What it does not do is provide the sports world with screaming headlines. Videos of players unloading duffel bags, walking into the complex in sunglasses and flip-flops, or playing long toss for the first time may send a slight shiver up the spine of the hardcore baseball fanatic, but it's not going to make people forget about the NBA, the NHL, or college basketball, which are all in the heat of their respective playoff drives.

Of course, there's always an exception to every rule, and 2020 was just that. Never before had the first day of spring training produced so many fireworks. The reason was that during the off-season it had been revealed that the Houston Astros had cheated during their 2017 championship season. They stole signs using a centerfield camera, a monitor in the tunnel just down the steps from the dugout, and a trash can lid that they banged on to let the batter know what pitch was coming. As sports crimes go, it was a whopper, calling into question the legitimacy of their World Series victory.

What I found fascinating was a Q and A that Astros owner Jim Crane did with the media. He'd had weeks to prepare for the moment. Weeks to prepare a statement and formulate answers to the questions the whole world knew were coming. How did he do?

By all accounts, not so hot.

Jeff Passan of ESPN wrote, "Amid his attempts at apologizing were clear signals that his contrition went only as far as his ability to absolve himself of wrongdoing. And the more Crane spoke, the more his words served as a spade, digging a hole from which he couldn't rescue himself."[17]

Alex Reimer of *Forbes* was no kinder: "Crane's flip-flop on the ramifications of his club's advanced sign-stealing methods was one of several excruciating and contradictory moments during his press conference Thursday."[18]

Adding to the outrage among fans and the media was the fact that the Astros' star players like Alex Bregman and Jose Altuve spoke for less that ninety seconds combined and didn't take any questions. The entire baseball world had been waiting for weeks to hear from the principals in what was arguably the biggest baseball scandal in one hundred years, and it seemed everyone walked away angry and dissatisfied. It's safe to say that the Astros are not going to win any popularity contests any time soon.

---

17 Jeff Passan, "What to Make of Houston Astros Owner Jim Crane's Public (Non-) Apology," ESPN, February 12, 2020, https://www.espn.com/mlb/story/_/id/28693762/what-make-houston-astros-owner-jim-crane-public-non-apology.

18 Alex Reimer, "Astros Owner Jim Crane Puts Disgraceful Bow On Cheating Scandal During Disastrous Press Conference," *Forbes* online, February 13, 2020, https://www.forbes.com/sites/alexreimer/2020/02/13/astros-owner-jim-crane-puts--disgraceful-bow-on-cheating-scandal-during-disastrous-press-conference/#5490e0261367.

All of which gives us some insight into what is one of the biggest challenges leaders face: taking the heat when something goes wrong. If you don't handle the situation well, the backlash can turn out to be as bad as the original problem. Or worse. The Astros are merely one in a long line of companies, organizations, and individuals that have had to do damage control after a disastrous turn of events. Some survive and some don't. Some actually enhance their standing by handling the situation with class while others, as in the case of Mr. Crane, pull out their gas can and pour fuel all over the fire. This is one of the biggest reasons why many people are reluctant to get into leadership. Taking the heat is hard. Doing a poor job of it can ruin you.

Why Leaders Make Good Targets

An old Far Side cartoon showed two deer standing in the forest having a conversation. One deer had what looked like a target on his side. The other deer was looking at it and said, "Bummer of a birthmark, Hal."

Leaders know what it's like to be Hal. They live every day of their lives with a target on them, for several reasons.

Reason #1: Leaders Are Decision-Makers

In *A Tale of Two Cities*, Charles Dickens wrote, "It was the best of times and the worst of times." Being a leader can easily put a person in the best of times or the worst of times, depending on how his or her decisions work out.

Richard Nixon, our thirty-seventh president, authorized a team to break into the Democratic campaign headquarters in the Watergate building in 1972. As decisions go, it was a bad one. But it wasn't half as bad as his next decision, which was to cover up the break-in. When Bob Woodward and Carl Bernstein, who were then young reporters for the *Washington Post*, started digging and uncovering alarming information, the White House scoffed and labeled their findings politics as usual, then secretly went into full cover-up mode. Eventually Nixon famously appeared on national TV and defended himself, claiming, "I am not a crook." But his was a house of cards. The truth is famous for worming its way toward the light in the same way a weed will worm its way through a slab of concrete. After the House Judiciary Committee passed three articles of impeachment, Nixon saw the handwriting on the wall and resigned the presidency on August 9, 1974.

But of course you don't have to be in the upper echelons of politics to become a target of criticism. Whether you teach school, manage a retail franchise, own a restaurant, or pastor a church, you will find your personal space being invaded by verbal projectiles if things don't go well. And yes, I'm sorry to say, even if it's not your fault.

The Richard Nixons of the world deserve the criticism they get, but lots of people in leadership are victims. They may uphold the highest standards of integrity, but if someone well down the chain of authority does something unethical, the leader will take the heat. The NCAA infractions committee likes to talk about a "lack of institutional control," which simply means the leader didn't do the crime but should have done more to prevent it. Unfortunately, even the greatest leader in the world can't know everything his or her subordinates are doing. Still, leaders are decision-makers and, for that reason alone, are going to take the heat.

Reason #2: It's Easier to Be Mad at One Person Than Many

Sometimes when bad things happen, there's plenty of blame to spread around. Take just about any problem in America, for example. Whose fault is it anyway?

There's always Congress, the legislative branch of government. Blaming Congress is easy because that's where laws are made. Congress makes good laws, of course. But it also makes bad laws, laws with loopholes, laws that go too far and other laws that don't go far enough.

Then, of course, there's the electorate, the people like you and me. If the Congress is doing a lousy job, shouldn't we be to blame? Didn't we vote those representatives and senators into office? Didn't we fall for their silver-tongued campaign promises? And beyond that, don't most problems the country faces originate with us? Isn't it citizens who drink and drive and rob convenience stores and use drugs and cheat on their taxes?

And what about the media? Just about everybody acknowledges that "fake news" is real. Time and time again, the media falls all over itself to push a narrative that turns out to be a fairy tale. Remember Michael Avenatti? Some segments of the media hailed him as a brilliant young attorney who could be the undoing of Donald Trump. He was interviewed on talk shows and news programs almost daily and praised to the heavens for his cunning. In the end he turned out to be a criminal who, as of this writing, is facing sentencing that could put him behind bars for forty years.

And then there's the Supreme Court. Every time they make a ruling, there is a segment of the population that feels an injustice has been done. Liberals and conservatives alike can point to Supreme Court decisions they despise.

But it's awfully exhausting to be mad at all of these people and institutions, isn't it? That's why most people just settle on the president. Sooner or later every leader comes to the place where he or she takes the heat by default.

Reason #3: Leaders Inspire Jealousy

If you're in a leadership position, you can be sure that somebody, somewhere wants your job. And when somebody wants your job, they are not going to sit back and talk about how wonderful you are. They are going to pick you apart and talk about all the things they would do differently if they were in charge. This is standard procedure in politics, of course. The challenger will never have a good word to say about the incumbent.

But even when someone doesn't actually want your job, he or she can be jealous of you. The simple fact that you are looked up to, in charge of something, or pulling down a nice salary can cause a person who doesn't have such things to feel a lot of angst. And again, the natural response is to nitpick and criticize.

I learned a long time ago that a good percentage of people would rather fret and stew about what they don't have than enjoy what they do have. As the old saying goes, when a man is unhappy because his crown doesn't shine as brightly as someone else's, he has two choices: he can polish his own crown or tarnish the other guy's. Lots of people choose to tarnish the other guy's. It's just easier.

Reason #4: Leaders Make People Angry

Or I should say, if they are doing their jobs right, they make people angry. Why? There are several reasons.

For one thing, part of a leader's job is to build a healthy culture, and that means insisting that people meet certain standards, like showing up on time. Showing up on time for work sounds like the easiest thing in the world, I know. But many people have trouble meeting even the most minimal standards of job performance. And when they don't, it's the leader's job to call them out and insist that they up their game.

Also, it's a leader's job to resolve conflict between team members. Let's face it, almost every person in America who's part of a team has a team member he or she doesn't care for. It might be someone with a gossipy tongue, someone who doesn't pull his share of the weight, someone who thinks he knows everything, someone whose laziness creates more work for everybody else. That type of situation is going to boil over sooner or later. When it does, the leader will have to step in and clean up the mess. Almost always, somebody walks away angry.

Finally, it's a leader's job to initiate change. Even if the order to change comes from up the leadership line, each leader at the various levels will be responsible for making sure the change happens. Those who don't like the change—and there are *always* those who don't like the change—will likely direct their ire toward the leader closest to them.

Yes, leaders make good targets, but leaders who know how to take the heat can thrive.

Obviously, the leader's personality and leadership style can minimize the amount of anger that is spurred by his or her actions, but it's never going to eliminate it altogether. I would say it's impossible to find a company anywhere that doesn't have former or current employees that are disgruntled or angry about one thing or another.

After reading this section, you might be thinking you never want to be a leader. Who wants to walk around with a target on his back? But it's not as bad as it sounds. Yes, leaders make good targets, but leaders who know how to take the heat can thrive.

How to Take the Heat without Melting Down

In the 1980s there was a deodorant called Dry Idea. One of their commercials showed a comedienne looking into the camera and saying, "There are three 'nevers' in comedy. Never follow a better comedian. Never let a heckler have the last word. And no matter how bad a joke bombs, never let them see you sweat."

I wish I could tell you that there's a deodorant you could pick up at your local store that would keep you cool when the heat's on. Unfortunately, it's not that easy. Taking the heat well requires some know-how. Let me give you a seven-step strategy.

Step #1: Evaluate the Criticism

Many years of leadership experience have taught me two things:

1. Most people believe the criticism leveled against them is illegitimate.
2. Most people are wrong.

However, that's not to say that all of the criticism we face is totally fair, or even that the majority of it is. A criticism can be accurate in a general sense and still be exaggerated. A preacher, for example, might be long-winded. It would be fair to say that his sermons ramble on too long. It probably would not be fair to say that he loves to hear the sound of his own voice and can't shut up. Or it might be true that a basketball coach's in-game demeanor toward referees is too aggressive. It likely would not be fair to say that he loses his mind if a call goes against his team.

People who criticize almost always embellish, which is why it's important for the person on the receiving end of the criticism to evaluate it carefully. (Isn't it strange how people who demonstrate no flair for oratory in everyday situations suddenly become masters of flowery hyperbole when criticizing someone?) I believe that most of the time, you're going to know in your heart if a criticism leveled against you is fair and accurate. If you honestly don't, talk to someone who loves you enough to tell you the truth.

The reason evaluating the criticism is so important is because it will determine your response. If you determine that the criticism is illegitimate or unfair, you will either ignore it or craft a response that sets the record straight. Very often ignoring it is the best idea, especially if you consider the source and judge it to be of minimal significance. Often people criticize out of their own smallness, and in such cases it's not worth the time or trouble to respond.

However, responding and setting the record straight is important if the criticism was made publicly and involves misinformation, or what is now called "fake news." Sticking up for yourself could salvage your reputation or in some cases your career, but at the very least it will let your critics know that you will not allow lies to go unchallenged.

On the other hand, if you know that the criticism you're getting is true and fair, I suggest you take the following steps.

Step #2: Be Honest

When President Clinton was first accused of sexual misconduct with Monica Lewinsky, his strategy was to deny, deny, deny. Then other women came forward with claims of more unsavory incidents. Again, the strategy was to deny, deny, deny. The result is that Bill Clinton, while a man of enormous ability and accomplishment, is a punch line for a thousand off-color sexual jokes. And the women who accuse him of misconduct still maintain their seething anger. One can't help wondering how differently he might be viewed if he'd only been honest about his mistakes and sought redemption.

There's simply nothing good that can come from trying to dodge the truth. Even if you're successful in the short term, it can come back to haunt you later. And when it does, the fallout will be greater than it would have been because at that point you will not only be known for the mistake you made but also for being a liar.

Never forget that when you tell a lie or cover up the truth, you are guaranteeing that whatever is causing you to take the heat isn't going away. When you lie today, you have to be on your guard tomorrow. You have to consider your words extra carefully so as not to contradict the story you told yesterday. The only way to put a mistake or a poor choice behind you is to tell the truth. You may have some fallout to deal with, but at least you can begin the process of restoring and repairing your life.

Let me give you two quick rules for being honest.

First, there's no such thing as halfway honesty. You're either honest or you aren't. The moment you decide to calculate which part of the truth you're going to tell and which part you're going to twist or cover up is the moment you decide to be dishonest.

And second, honesty helps you most when it is voluntary. Getting caught and *then* coming clean is always a bad look. People will withhold any sympathy they might have given you because they'll figure your confession was forced upon you instead of willingly chosen.

Step #3: Don't Make Excuses

Excuse-making goes all the way back to the Garden of Eden. When God confronted Adam about eating the forbidden fruit, Adam said, in essence, "I did, but that woman you gave me made me do it. It was all her idea. I would have been fine if she hadn't come along and tempted me." And people have been making excuses ever since.

I've lived long enough to have heard just about every excuse there is.

I was afraid.

I was lonely.

I was misled.

I was framed.

I was desperate for money.

I wasn't given a fair chance.

I didn't have time to prepare.

I didn't have all the information.

The dog ate my homework.

At the beginning of this chapter, I mentioned the Houston Astros sign-stealing scandal. One of the players, in attempting to explain why he had participated and had not tried to stop the practice, said that he had gotten swept along by the momentum of the thing. It was what a person might say if he accidentally fell out of a white-water rafting canoe and was swept along by the rapids. Only there was nothing accidental about the sign-stealing, and the player could have chosen to stop at any time. Hence, the statement came off sounding like a lame excuse and drew the ire of fans and media alike.

If being less than honest is the worst thing a leader can do when the heat is on, making excuses is the second worst. Excuses make a leader look weak, like a victim rather than strong and in control. And here's the irony: most leaders do not want to hear excuses from the people who work for them. Coaches I've known have had practice shirts printed with the words "No Excuses." Yet some of those same leaders will resort to excuses when the heat gets turned up on them.

Now, you may be thinking, "But what if there are legitimate reasons for what went wrong? Shouldn't I be able to state those in my defense?" My advice is simply to take responsibility when the heat is on and not try to explain your way out of the situation because what seems to you like a reasonable explanation will sound to others like whining. If you're the leader and something bad happened on your watch, just own it. Over time mitigating factors may surface and work to your benefit by bringing greater understanding. But when the heat is on, you'll lose respect if you even appear to be making excuses.

Step #4: Apologize When It's Appropriate

Sounds easy, right?

It isn't, apparently.

I never cease to be amazed at the number of people who make a mess of their apology. When Matt Lauer was busted for extreme sexual misconduct in the workplace, he said, "Some of what is being said about me is untrue or mischaracterized, but there is enough truth in these stories to make me feel embarrassed and ashamed." In other words, "I am a victim too. Those mean women who accused me didn't get the details just right." All of America cringed when that one hit the airwaves.

HuffPost writer Caroline Bologna wrote a piece about apologizing that made some excellent points.[19] One of the things she pointed out is that any apology that fails to focus on your own behavior is a bad apology. For example, "I'm sorry you feel that way" is one of the all-time worst things you can say. Close behind it is "I'd like to apologize if I offended anyone." With such statements you're implying

---

19 Caroline Bologna, "The Biggest Mistakes People Make When Apologizing," HuffPost, July 30, 2018, https://www.huffpost.com/entry/biggest-apology-mistakes_n_5b575e3ce4b0de86f4910f69.

that the problem isn't what you said or did but how other people are reacting to it. When you apologize, talk about your own words or actions and why they were wrong. Anything else you mention will probably only undermine your apology and make it seem cheap and insincere.

One other thing about apologizing: Do it quickly. A late apology will seem like it was given as a last resort, as if you didn't really want to do it but had to. That in itself could leave a bad taste in people's mouths.

Step #5: Don't Throw Others under the Bus

As the leader you are going to have all the inside scoop. You're going to know who on your team was responsible for helping to bring about the failure. Human nature will make you want to reference that information in your apology. Don't do it. Handle individual failures behind closed doors, for two reasons. One, the public doesn't care about the inner workings of your company or organization; the public only cares about results. And two, if you throw your own people under the bus, they will resent it. And the last thing you want is for your own people to resent you. Instead, let them know that you have their backs even when they mess up. That's one of the best ways to build loyalty.

Step #6: Move On

Many leaders make the mistake of talking too much about what went wrong. I'm not saying you shouldn't say everything that needs to be said, I'm simply saying that once you *have* said everything that needs to be said, you should let it go and move on. Hashing and rehashing things over and over again accomplishes nothing.

However, this is what your detractors will want you to do. Those who don't like you or support you will want you to keep having to deal with the problem. If there's someone who wants your job, he or she will be only too happy for you to sit on the hot seat for as long as possible. Somebody said, "The more you stir the pot, the more it stinks." You can be sure your enemies will stir the pot. It will be up to you to figure out the appropriate time to stop answering questions and move on.

Step #7: Take Steps to Ensure the Failure Won't Happen Again

Oddly enough, this is the step a lot of people overlook.

There is a restaurant in Central Florida that has been closed down by the health department numerous times. Most of the locals who live near it know of its history and avoid it, but the tourists have no clue, so they keep it in business. What's crazy is that the place never seems to get its act together. It corrects whatever violations the inspector finds so that it can reopen its doors but apparently never conquers the systemic issues that drag it down.

A surprising number of businesses and organizations are this way, and I'm not talking about little one-horse operations. Take the New England Patriots, for example. How many times in recent years have they been caught breaking some kind of rule? There was "Spygate," "Snowplowgate," and "Deflategate," to name a few. Ask any football fan who is not a Patriots' fan, and you will find a high level of irritation spurred by the team's seeming inability to stop breaking rules.

As a leader you can't ensure that there will never be a failure in your organization. You can't monitor every employee all the time. But when something bad happens and the heat is on, you can and must figure out what went wrong and fix it. That might mean firing people.

It might mean coming up with some new policies or procedures. Keep in mind that most people won't blame you for a mistake. Who hasn't made mistakes? But they will blame you for harboring a culture that allows the same mistakes to keep happening.

When I think about taking the heat, I'm reminded that heat is an essential part of the process of refining gold. In my experience, heat refines people too. There are exceptions, as I just mentioned, but for the most part, when something goes wrong and the heat is turned up, people learn and become better. When you were a kid, your parents disciplined you. They turned up the heat (perhaps on the seat of your pants) to impress upon you the importance of changing your behavior. And chances are you did.

Well, nothing has changed. The heat will still get turned up now and then, only this time it won't be your parents doing the turning. The heat will, however, give you the same chance to learn and grow, to be refined as a person and a leader. This is why I tell reluctant leaders not to be afraid of the heat. It can only hurt you if you are stubborn and thickheaded.

When I think about taking the heat, I'm reminded that heat is an essential part of the process of refining gold. In my experience, heat refines people too.

CHAPTER 10

Ready to Launch

I'm hoping that by now you have overcome your reluctance to lead, that you have seen how all the concerns you have are manageable. But you still might not be ready to jump into a leadership role. That's what this last chapter is about—making sure you're prepared to take that step. I want to share with you something that I have come to understand over the course of my career that I believe will help you reach your potential as a leader. It's not a list of dos and don'ts but rather an overview of the indispensable qualities that make any leader successful.

Isn't it true that in just about every area of life there are indispensable qualities that make a person successful? For example, all great baseball pitchers change speeds, move the ball around, and throw strikes. They *all* do; it doesn't matter how hard they throw, whether they're righthanded or lefthanded, or whether they start or relieve.

Likewise, every great leader possesses certain identifiable qualities. It doesn't matter if he leads a small country church or a multinational corporation; if he does it well, you will see these qualities in play. And these qualities are not new. You can go back to the time of Moses or Solomon and you'll see them in full view. You could drop in on George Washington or Abraham Lincoln or, closer in time, Steve Jobs or Jack Welch. Examine any great leader in any generation and you will observe these qualities.

I came to identify and understand them in three basic ways: by reading hundreds of books about leadership, by observing great leaders around me, and by living the life of a leader myself. One day, after many years of living in the leadership world and continuing to feed my mind, they just seemed to crystallize. It's like when you grow up in a house full of beautiful paintings: you walk past them a thousand times. You see them, but you don't *really* see them. Then one day it's as if the scales fall from your eyes and there they are, speaking to you in ways they never did before. From that moment on, you love those paintings and realize how precious they are.

Once I identified these qualities, they became the lens through which I viewed leadership and the foundation of all my teaching on leadership. I believe every leader should memorize them and review them often. If you have trouble memorizing, then tape them to the bathroom mirror or to your computer screen—any place where you will be reminded of them often. They will keep you on course as your leadership life unfolds and various challenges come across your path. They will never fail you.

So here they are—seven qualities that will make you a great leader.

Quality #1: Vision

What is vision in the leadership sense? It's having a clear, inspiring, challenging sense of where you want to take your team or organization. Simply put, it's being able to see what others cannot see.

There is a story about Abraham Lincoln that is a perfect example of what I'm talking about. At a critical point in the Civil War, the Union general George Meade won a victory over Robert E. Lee at Gettysburg. As Lee and his forces were retreating, Meade was slow in chasing him, which allowed Lee to escape with most of his army intact. To put a positive spin on his blunder, Meade boasted that he had chased "every vestige of the invader from our soil." When Lincoln heard this, he was furious. He shouted, "Drive the invader from our soil? Will our generals never get the idea? The *whole country* is our soil!"

Everything Lincoln did as president was based on his vision of America as one, whole, undivided country. As we sit here today, that seems like a nice thought. But it doesn't take much imagination to realize that if Lincoln hadn't had such a vision for America, our world could look very different today. For example, if America had been divided into two much less powerful countries, would World War II have turned out differently? Truly, the possibilities are frightening. But Abraham Lincoln's vision and his relentless drive to see it become a reality prevented any such disastrous scenarios.

One of the keys to developing a vision is to constantly ask yourself, "What if?" There are two ways this question can help you.

First, it can help you look beyond what you're currently doing. Sometimes we get so comfortable with our current policies and procedures that we fail to think outside the box. It's the old "If it ain't broke, don't fix it" mentality. But even if something isn't "broke," there might still be a better way to do it. Developments in technology are constantly bringing new tools into play, and original thinkers across the country are producing effective innovations. But those new tools and ideas will slip past you unnoticed if you're not constantly asking, "What if?"

Second, a "What if?" mentality will help you anticipate trends that could impact your business. Visionary leaders understand that the current cultural climate, no matter what it is, will not last forever. There is a new big thing coming, and maybe sooner than you think. Frequently asking, "What if this happens?" or "What if that happens?" is a good way to keep from ending up one of those organizations that operates behind the curve and, therefore, never reaches its potential.

I am often credited with bringing the Orlando Magic to Central Florida. In truth, there were a lot of people involved in making it happen. The reason my name comes up in the discussion is not because I did everything but because I was one of the first to catch the vision. The question "What if we had an NBA franchise in Orlando?" didn't seem ridiculous to me. I was able to picture it, and from there began to talk about it and describe it. The next thing I knew, people were getting excited, and today that vision is a reality.

Vision is where it all starts. What do you see when you close your eyes and think about the future of your business or organization? Whatever it is, let it guide you as you make your decisions.

Quality #2: Communication

It stands to reason that the greatest vision in the world will mean little if it isn't communicated well. No one on your team will know what your vision is, understand it, or get excited about it until you are able to plant it in their hearts and minds.

And quite honestly this is where a lot of leaders fail.

Many leaders take on the role of a bureaucrat. They plop themselves down in an office behind a desk and start issuing edicts and firing off emails and memos. If something goes haywire, they might yell and pound the desk or fire somebody, but that's about it. Meanwhile, the rank and file members of the organization continue to work like automatons with no greater goal in mind than drawing their next paycheck. They don't see the big picture. They don't have a clue where the company is headed because no one has told them. They are, quite literally, just going through the motions.

At some point people need to be inspired, and inspiration comes through communication. But there's more to communication than you might think. It's not just talking. Have you ever known a person who talked all the time and never said anything? Political candidates are especially bad about this. They often resort to meaningless platitudes and clichés that make nice soundbites but don't really mean anything.

A few years ago, I interviewed Bob Sheppard for a book I was doing about public speaking. Bob was the public address announcer for the New York Yankees from 1951 until 2007. His distinctive introductions became so iconic that Reggie Jackson nicknamed him "The Voice of God." Apart from his duties with the Yankees, Bob was a college speech instructor. When I asked him to share with me his keys to effective communication, he said, "Be clear, be concise, and be correct."

Be clear. In other words, learn to communicate your vision in a way that every person on your team can understand. Don't ramble, don't use big words, don't veer off topic, and above all don't be cryptic. If somebody on your team walks away after listening to you and says, "What did he mean when he said … ?" you have failed.

Be concise. Never use ten words to say what you could say using five. Never take a page to say what you could say in a paragraph. Figure out what is the least number of words it would take to communicate your vision, and use that number. People's eyes start to glaze over when you go on and on. The more words you use, the harder it is to communicate well.

Be correct. If you establish a pattern of having to eat your words or retract your statements or issue corrections or apologies, people will quickly start tuning you out. Make absolutely sure something is true before you say it. And when you make a promise, make sure you keep it.

Over the years I have learned that everything works better when good communication is happening. Husbands and wives know this very well. So do doctors and patients, teachers and students, players and coaches, candidates and constituents, preachers and parishioners, and yes, team leaders and team members.

Quality #3: People Skills

I've known former NBA coach Phil Jackson for many years. His eleven championship rings tell you that he knew what he was doing as a leader. Because a number of his former players wore Magic jerseys, I got to hear them tell stories about his manner of dealing with people. One thing that stands out in my mind is that at Christmas time Phil would buy books and other gifts for his players. But he wouldn't just buy fifteen copies of the same book and give one to every player. He actually bought a different book for every player, depending on what he thought each player would like or find helpful. What a tremendous example of people skills!

And then there's Dick Vermeil. I was the general manager of the Philadelphia 76ers when he was the coach of the Eagles. His office at Veterans Stadium was near our facility. One day I was talking to Ron Jaworski, who quarterbacked the Eagles in their heyday. He said, "If you ever played for Dick Vermeil, you'd better count on getting phone calls from him for the rest of your life. He'll usually call you around dinnertime, and he'll be calling to see how you're doing."

But perhaps my favorite story is about Andy Reid. During the month of November of his Super Bowl–winning season with the Kansas City Chiefs, he did something almost unthinkable. I was in Philadelphia to emcee the induction ceremony for the Philadelphia Sports Hall of Fame. One of the inductees, former Eagles quarterback Donavon McNabb, stood at the podium thanking a number of people who were instrumental in his success. During his remarks, he said, "And I want to thank my former coach, Andy Reid, for being here."

I looked around, and sure enough, there was Andy sitting not far away. I couldn't help thinking what a sacrifice he had made to be there in the middle of a hotly contested season. The Chiefs had no doubt had practice that day, which meant that Andy had jumped on a private jet to take him to Philly in time for the banquet and then reboarded the plane to fly back to Kansas City after the banquet. Very few people would do something like that.

These stories about three great coaches make it clear that leaders who have great people skills care about people. Genuinely care about them. These coaches didn't see their players as mere tools in a toolbox or as chess pieces on a board to be moved here and there as needed. They were real people with hearts and souls and minds.

I once asked Seth Greenburg, a longtime college basketball coach and current ESPN analyst, how a coach can get his players to play hard for him. Seth said, "Oh, that's not hard at all."

I was surprised and said, "It's not? I would think that would be the hardest part of coaching."

"Not at all," he said. "If you care about your players as human beings, if they know you *really* care, believe me, they'll play hard for you. In fact, they'll run through walls for you."

One of the best examples of caring about people comes from my old boss, Rich DeVos. In 1997 we had an RDV Sports meeting in

Grand Rapids, Michigan. Mr. DeVos, who was the owner, was still recovering from a heart transplant but joined us via teleconferencing.

The first order of business was the need to downsize the Magic Fan Attic team store. Sixteen jobs had to be eliminated. We debated and discussed the job for twenty minutes or so, and then Rich spoke up: "This funeral has gone on long enough. It's time for the burial." But to him, the move wasn't just about saving money. It was about people. He said, "Those sixteen employees who are losing their jobs . . . I want them taken care of. Either relocate them in the organization, or give them good severance checks, or help them find jobs, but I want them taken care of. Understood?"

Oh, yes, we all understood.

And here's the best part of that story: Rich didn't know any of those sixteen people, but he truly cared about them because they were members of his team.

Just by caring about the people you're leading you will increase your chances of success many times over.

Quality #4: Character

Your character is the array of personality traits you have built into your life over time. These traits determine how you will behave in a range of situations, including times of pressure, danger, stress, and temptation. I am always amused when I hear some high-profile person who has gotten caught in some sort of scandal try to explain himself. He often says, "This is not who I am. Such behavior is very out of character for me. I was just under a lot of pressure." The person is saying, in other words, that his character stands up just fine until pressure comes, and then it falls apart. I would counter with this simple truth: you can tell people what kind of character you have, but they will see it for themselves when pressure comes. Pressure *reveals* your character.

> **You can tell people what kind of character you have, but they will see it for themselves when pressure comes. Pressure *reveals* your character.**

Stories about the character of great leaders abound. One of my favorites is about the late Pat Summitt, the legendary women's basketball coach at the University of Tennessee. When she started coaching, she made $250 a month—a *month*—and had numerous duties in addition to coaching, including washing the team uniforms and driving the team van. Many people—perhaps the majority—would complain to high heaven about such a situation. Not Pat. She simply knuckled down and did the work. That's character.

Of all the qualities that make a great leader, character is the one that will help you build a great legacy. There are lots of people who can point to professional accomplishments, but we don't respect them as much as you might think because those accomplishments are tainted by gross lapses in character. In recent years we've seen a whole string of powerful, accomplished men be publicly shamed because of their atrocious treatment of women. In fact, on the very day that these words are being written, Harvey Weinstein, the movie mogul, has been found guilty of horrific sexual crimes against women and will potentially spend decades behind bars. Though his professional accomplishments are considerable, at this point nobody cares. His character has doomed his legacy.

By contrast, think about Billy Graham. Over the seven-decade history of the Billy Graham Evangelistic Association, there has never been a hint of scandal surrounding the leadership of that organization. Other religious leaders and organizations have had scandals of the tawdriest nature. Many have lost their ministries and their reputations, but not Billy Graham. Why? Because the leadership circle of that organization made a commitment to build moral firewalls between themselves and temptation.

While Harvey Weinstein was recklessly pursuing pleasure without regard to the pain he might cause others, Billy Graham was pursuing purity. A comparison of the results is striking, but the difference is not as huge as you might think. They were both smart, capable men in their respective fields. It all boils down to a difference in character.

Quality #5: Competence

A few years ago, I wrote a book called *Coaching Your Kids to Be Leaders.* As a part of my research for that book, I sent a questionnaire to leaders across the country and asked, "Are leaders born or made?" About 85 percent of the respondents replied that leaders are made, which was good news for me. If they had said leaders are born, I would have had to call my publisher and say, "Never mind. There's no need to write this book."

I like the story about a group of tourists passing through a picturesque village. They saw a group of men sitting together by a fence. One of the tourists asked, "Were any great men born in this village?" The oldest man answered, "No, only babies."

And it's true. Only babies are born. Then begins the process of learning and developing. Those who grow up to become leaders will do so by developing competencies. Here are three that are important for leaders.

Competency #1: Problem-Solving

The leader's lap is where problems eventually end up. They may be talked about and analyzed in the break room or the cafeteria or down at the local Starbucks, but they're eventually going to end up in the leader's lap. And there they will meet their doom if the leader is a problem-solver.

Let me just say that problem-solving brings a lot of satisfaction. When something is wrong and you help make it right, that's a great feeling. It's also one of the best ways to win the confidence of your team. Being a problem-solver gives you credibility like almost nothing else can.

Competency #2: Selling

You've heard the term "buying in."

A basketball announcer might say, "The players have really bought in to the coach's defense-first philosophy."

A political analyst might say, "The electorate is starting to buy in to the candidate's ideas about healthcare."

A parent might say, "I finally got my teenager to buy in to the idea of getting a job."

The right people buying in to a great concept or philosophy is often a prerequisite to a business's or organization's success. Without buy-in, there's a disconnect. Team members end up pulling in different directions, which means success will be hard to come by, which means everybody will be frustrated. Buy-in is critical.

But buy-in doesn't happen unless some effective selling happens first. Sometimes the idea of being a "salesman" is met with an eye roll, and not without reason. But the truth is that salesmen often make great leaders. Getting your people to believe in your ideas and philosophy brings so many great things within reach.

Competency #3: Team-Building

If you follow the news, you know that our country is very divided. There are racial, economic, educational, political, and spiritual differences that sometimes boil over into some pretty ugly behaviors. However, if you look at the typical sports team, you'll see people of all kinds, colors, backgrounds, and political viewpoints working together, encouraging each other, rooting for each other, and celebrating victories with hugs and high fives. This is the beauty of teams. Teams break down walls like almost nothing else can. Coach Bill Curry, who started the Georgia State University football program, has called it "the miracle of the huddle."

This is why it's critical for a leader to be a team-builder. The ability to take a collection of individuals and turn them into one well-oiled unit makes great accomplishments possible. In fact, sport teaches us that the best collection of talent often doesn't win. How many times have you heard an announcer say, "On paper, they're not as good, but they play well together as a team"? Wise leaders work hard every day to pull their people together, to build unity, and to make them realize how much they depend on each other.

Quality #6: Boldness

One of the boldest things I ever did as a leader was recommend to the owner of the Philadelphia 76ers that he should spend $6 million to acquire Julius Erving from the New York Nets. That was $3 million to the Nets and $3 million to sign Dr. J to a new contract. I know what you're thinking: "Six million dollars? That's not a lot of money when you're talking about sports salaries." Oh, but dear reader, this happened in 1976. Back then $6 million was an enormous sum. I remember when I first heard the number, my jaw almost came unhinged. Some would have said I was crazy for making such a recommendation to our owner. But if you know your NBA history, you know it was the key move that took us to the next level and brought Philadelphia an NBA championship in 1983.

Boldness is often the thing that separates a leader, a company, an organization, or a team from the next level. The basic pieces may be there, but perhaps one more daring move is what's needed to go over the top. One of the challenges of being bold is that there will always be small thinkers around trying to scare you into standing pat.

The key to being bold is to gather the facts and then decide. But don't wait until you have every fact because you will probably never get them all. Lee Iacocca used to say that if he made a decision with 75 percent of the available facts, he rarely regretted it. The poor leaders are the ones that sit on the fence because they lack some little piece of information. And while they're sitting, the window of opportunity closes.

If you're a baseball fan, the name Cornelius McGillicuddy probably doesn't ring a bell. However, the name he went by—Connie Mack—probably does. Connie Mack managed the Philadelphia Athletics for the first fifty years of their existence. The members of that team were my boyhood idols. Connie used to say, "You can't grind grain with water that has already gone down the creek." Sounds weird in this age of high-tech machinery, but what he was saying is that if you miss an opportunity, it's gone forever.

Of course, some of your bold moves won't work out. All great leaders can look back on decisions they made that went bust. But it's better to make a few bad moves if it means you can make some great ones too. The great ones will more than offset the bad ones. In fact, people won't even remember the bad ones if you make a few great ones. But one thing is certain—you'll never make *any* great moves if you lead out of fear.

Quality #7: A Serving Heart

In the Bible you have story after story about people defying great odds, stepping up to face seemingly invincible enemies, or performing heroic acts on blood-soaked battlefields. But for me, the most significant leadership act in the Bible happened among a handful of men in a quiet room far from the flaming projectiles and murderous threats of a charging enemy. It was not an act of heroism but of humility. It was the evening Jesus took a towel and a basin of water and knelt before his disciples to wash their feet.

There is, of course, a "yuck" factor involved in such an act, especially when you stop to consider how dirty people's feet were in those days. Nike and Reebok were still a couple of millennia in the future, and pedicures had yet to catch on. Not to mention the fact that people walked everywhere they went in sandals on dusty roads. You could wash your feet and one minute after you walked out your front door, your feet would be dirty again. Imagine what they must have been like at the end of a long day.

> If you want the love and respect of your people—which is critical if you want to be a leader—you can't fake it. You've got to be a real, honest-to-goodness servant.

But Jesus's main concern wasn't that his disciples had the cleanest feet in town. His concern was that they saw an example of servant leadership, that they knew what it meant to be humble, to stoop and do the dirty work. He knew that he was going to leave those guys in charge of leading the infant church. He knew it was critical that the church get off to a good start, that it be led well. The one thing he didn't want was for his disciples to be cocky and arrogant and all about themselves. He wanted them to realize that they were going to set the tone with their attitudes and behaviors. So he made sure they saw a vivid example of what it means to be both a leader and a servant.

Sam Walton, the founder of Walmart, was well known as a servant leader. It is said that he never asked a Walmart employee to do anything he wasn't willing to do himself. And his spirit of humility wasn't just an act. He was often seen working right alongside his hourly wage employees. In fact, near the end of his life, when he was lying in a hospital bed taking chemotherapy, he wasn't in a hospital. His bed was actually in his Walmart office because he wanted to be near his people. It's no wonder he was so beloved.

If you want the love and respect of your people—which is critical if you want to be a leader—you can't fake it. You've got to be a real, honest-to-goodness servant.

And so we come to the end of this book. It's my hope that the reluctance you were feeling when you picked it up has all gone, that you now understand that every fear you had has an appropriate "fix" and that the seven essential qualities of a great leader are well within your reach. I am of the opinion that there is a vast reservoir of leadership ability in this world that has never been tapped. People are walking around everywhere who could do amazing things in leadership but have never tried, in many cases because they shy away from opportunities.

Stop shying away.

Stop making excuses.

Stop selling yourself short.

Stop allowing your hesitation to hold you back.

Somewhere near you—in your church, your neighborhood, your school district, your local charity—a leader is needed. Now is your time.

Get out there and lead!

ABOUT MARK ATTEBERRY

Mark Atteberry is the award-winning author of twelve books, including *The Samson Syndrome* and *The Solomon Seduction*. He lives in Central Florida with his wife, Marilyn. Learn more about him at alittlestrongereveryday.com.

CONTACT INFORMATION

If you would like to contact Pat, he can be reached at pwilliams@patwilliams.com. His phone number is 407-721-0922.

If you are interested in booking Pat for a speaking engagement or interview, contact Andrew Herdliska at 407-969-7578.

Printed in the USA
CPSIA information can be obtained
at www.ICGtesting.com
JSHW012031140824
68134JS00033B/2991